AF568113

COGNITIVE ARCHITECTURE IN VISUALLY IMPAIRED

By

Dr. Anita Julka

Reader

Dept. of Education of Groups
with Sepeical Needs
NCERT
New Delhi

DISCOVERY PUBLISHING HOUSE
NEW DELHI-110002

Reprinted - 2018

First Published - 2006

ISBN: 978-81-8356-049-8

Cognitive Architecture in Visually Impaired

Published by:

DISCOVERY PUBLISHING HOUSE PVT. LTD.
4383/4B, Ansari Road, Darya Ganj
New Delhi-110 002 (India)
Phone: +91-11-23279245, 43596064-65
Fax: +91-11-23253475
E-mail: discoverypublishinghouse@gmail.com
sales@discoverypublishinggroup.com
web: www.discoverypublishinggroup.com

Printed at:
Infinity Imaging Systems
Delhi

Preface

The emergence of cognitive science has opened up new research vistas and shifts in paradigm. For instance, thus issue raised by faculty theorists who stress the role of specific principles underlying a specific situation like the distinction between short-term store and long-term store have been re-phased in the frame work of cognitive science. Unitary approach holds that all the higher level cognitive functions are realised by one of the principles constitutes another issue which is a focus of an active debate in cognitive science. Psychologists, in the framework of cognitive science have carried out experiments to theorize about cognitive functions using the faculty approach. Anderson (1983), Klahr, Langley and Neches (1987) and others have based their studies of cognitive functions on unitary approach, using the term "cognitive architecture" defined as complete proposals about the structure of human cognition contrasting with theories which address only one aspect of psychology by Newell, is the production system framework, successfully employed as programmes for computer simulation in studying acquisition of cognitive skills, specific tasks like Tower of Hanaoi, Balance-Scale, etc., also used in comparing expert-novice behaviour in terms of conditions-action rules called production rules. These rules, as approaches to the study of cognitive architecture, have the advantage of being homogeneous, independent, flexible, goal-directed, and their good structuring helps guarantee production of coherent behaviour.

No study has so far been carried out to analyse cognitive architecture in the visually impaired, to bring out the distinctive features of their cognitive processing. The differences in the production rules used by expert and novice in terms of content and complexities of the rules they produced, and the advantage of production rule framework to lend itself for training and learning purposes as shown by the intelligent—tutoring systems led to the idea of studying the cognitive architecture in the visually impaired using production system. In their circumstances of getting segmentary inputs from other modalities, in the absence of vision and then trying to integrate this information to deal with their environment leads to segregation based on the fact, that they are not as well informed as the sighted who get a global picture of the whole world with all the senses intact. One way of bringing the visually impaired at par with the sighted population in order to integrate them in the community would be to provide them with all the information related to the world through some other means so that they can cognitively process the various skills and tasks in varied domains, as successfully as the sighted. Production rules were considered to the appropriate therefore, in the study of not only the cognitive architecture but also in finding how training provided using this framework, can help the visually impaired to equate themselves with the sighted in the processing and solving of various tasks which formed the framework of this society. The present study makes an humble attempt in this direction.

Many people and organizations contributed to this research. I wish to express my sincere gratitude and thanks to my guide/supervisor, Professor G.C. Gupta, who gave me an opportunity to work under him and saw me through the whole process that culminated in the present work. Without his expert guidance, this work would not have been possible as there were no guidelines from research literature, this research being a pioneer effort in this field.

I am thankful to Professor (Dr.) K.D. Broota, Head of the Department of Psychology for his help, interest and guidance to the research from time to time.

My special thanks are also due to Mr. A.K. Mittal, Principal, J.P.M. School for the blind, for his cooperation in the implementation of the research, by allowing me to use the library facility and to test the visually impaired subjects for as many days as I wished.

I am also thankful to the principles of all the other schools covered in this research, for their excellent support which facilitated my work considerably.

I also take this opportunity to express my appreciation to Dr. B.S. Nagi, Senior Research Fellow Cum-Senior System Manager, Council for Social Development, for his immense help in computer analysis and processing of data.

The staff of the Department of Psychology were also very cooperative which made my work easier.

I am equally thankful to Mr. Hemant Deoliya for painstaking typing of the manuscript and providing secretarial support to the study.

The subject of the study, particularly the visually impaired ones, deserve my special thanks. Their excellent support was available whenever the study required.

Last, but not the least, I would like to thank my family for the support and help they provided in various ways during the whole study period.

(Anita Julka)

Contents

Preface

1. Introduction 1
2. Problem and Objectives 35
3. Methodology 39
4. Results 58
5. Discussion, Limitations and Suggestions for Further Research 110
6. Summary 121

References *126*

Index *145*

1

Introduction

Concepts

A traditional pre-experimental view of the mind is that it divides into three domains. Conation (the action of the will), affect (the action of emotions) and cognition (the action of the intelleot). By and 1arge, it would be true if we said that Cognitive Psychology and the associated discipline of the Cognitive Science have at their core the study of the actions of the intellect.

The use of computer as a model for theories of human intellect rose to prominence in the seminal book by Miller, Galanter and Pribram (1960). Newell & Simon (1972) in their book Human Problem Solving' gave a computational account of problem solving establishing a firm link between the view that Artificial Intelligence should strive to imitates human cognition and the view that computer simulations afford testable theoretical models of cognitive processes.

The computational view of thought views thinking as the manipulation of an internal representation of an external domain expressed in some internal language (mental model) called mentalese by Fodor (1975). Newell (1980) & Pylyshyn (1984) define three distinct levels of psychological theory within a computational view. **Information Processing** theories attempt to define human mentalese and the machine associated with it. **Physical Theories** explain how the mentalese machine is instantiated by the brain.

Representational Theories expresses regularities in the way that relationships in the external world are captured by mental models.

Cognitive Architecture

Cognitive architecture, one important concept ualization that emerged as a consequence of these analyses of mind has caught the imagination of quite a few cognitive scientists, Anderson (1983) being one such Cognitive Scientist. Earl Hunt (1989) defined system architecture in terms of primitive operations available to manipulate mentalese date structure and how they fit together. Pylyshyn in (1984) in 'Computation and Cognition', has stated, that the biological factors interact with symbol level generalizations by causing modifications in the basic computational resources. This is called the functional architecture. The functional architecture of the system provides the computational resources for realizing cognitive processes, Just as a computer's "virtual machine" or programming language provides the resources for realizing running computer programs.

Thus, the classical architectures of the mind postulates representational mental states committed to a symbol level of representation or to a language of, thought combining the syntactic and semantic structures.

The concept of symbol, according to Newell & Simon (1972) is a set of elements or tokens (instances or occurrences) connected by a set of relations forming the symbol structure. The figure (taken from Newell and Simon 1972) shows the general characteristics of the information Processing system as a proposed by Newell and Simon.

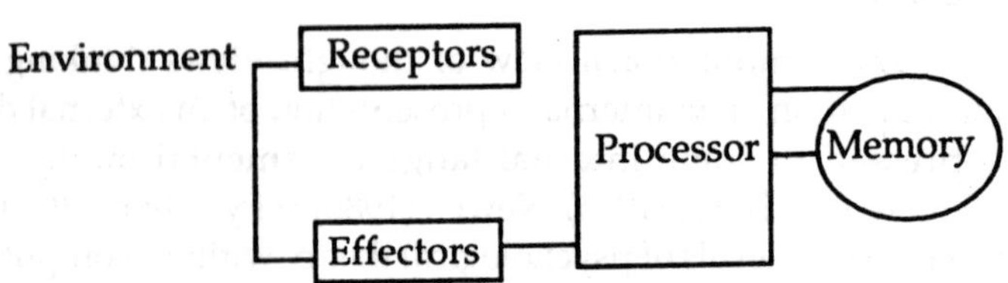

Fig.1.1 Information processing system

Thus, Newell and Simon, in their classical picture of a general structure of processing system suggested not only symbols and symbol structures but also a memory, a component of an information processing system capable of storing and retaining symbol structures. A processor, consisting of a) set of elementary information processes (EIP's); b) a short-term memory (STM) that holds the input output symbol structures of the EIP, and c) and interpreter, that determines the sequences of EIP's to be executed by the IPS as a function of the symbol structures in STM.

Classical models of the mind were derived from the structure of Turing & Von Neuman machines. The Turing machine as conceptualized by Allan Turing (1936) was considered to be able to compute all functions which were conceived to be computable. Later around 1945, John Von Neuman model of computer set the stage for the advent of Artificial Intelligence. The typical architecture of Von Neumann machine (control, storage, input and output units) contributed to the understanding of cognition and further development in the field of computer, made it clear that the basic idea derived from these machines, is not related to the physical structure of the computer or hardware but to the functional architecture as determined by the software constraint, such as operating system and programming language. But the idea of a modular organization of the mind (Fodor 1989) according to which, modules are self—contained, automatically functioning components of the system, which may have a physical representation in the brain as supported by studies of the effects of brain damage on language competence has made cognitive scientists to retain the hardware analogy to some extent.

Thus, as stated by J.A. Fodor and Z.W. Pylyshyn (1988) the architecture of the cognitive system consists of the set of basic operations, resources, functions, principles etc. (generally the sorts of properties that would be described in a "user's manual" for the architecture if it were available on the computer) whose domain and range are the representational status of the organism.

The domain of the cognition can be studied, according to J.R. Anderson (1983), using two approaches. The Faculty approach holds that distinct cognitive principles underlie the operation of distinct cognitive functions (Boxing, 1950). On the contrary **Unitary** approach holds that all higher—level cognitive functions can be explained by one set of principles.

The unitary approach is evident in the early S-R theories and presently has found an important representation in the modern general purpose computer, in symbolic programming languages which showed how a single set of principles could explain a broad range of computational tasks.

As stated by Newell (1972) "Even if the mind has parts, mtdules, components or whatever, they all mesh together to produce behaviour, it is one mind that minds them all". Unitary approach was taken by Newell, his colleague Simon and computer scientist Clifford Shaw in their pioneering work on human problem solving back in 1950's and 1960's.' Newell and Simon developed a program known as General Problem Solver in 1957, as a model for human problem solving, following the unitary approach to study cognition. Other programs following the Unitary approach are The

General Problem Solver Programs of Fikes and Nilsson (1971), Sacerdoti (1977) and General Inference systems (Green & Raphael 1969; McDermott & Doyle, 1980) and General Scheme Systems (Bobrow & Wiiiograd, 1977; Minsky 1977; Rumeihart and Ortony, 1986; Schank & Abelson, 1977).

All these programs or systems are theories of human cognition because they are cognitive architectures. Cognitive architectures, according to Anderson (1993) are relatively comple⁺ⁿ proposals about the structure of human cognition.

The term cognitive architecture was brought into psychology by Newell (1967), from his work on computer architectures. Jusj as an architect tries to provide a complete specification of a house (for a builder) so a computer or cognitive architecture tries to provide a complete specification of a system. There is abstraction in a cognitive or computer architecture. One does not specify the exact neurons in a cognitive architecture and one does not specify the exact computing elements in a computer architecture.

Production System Architecture

Production system is another example of unitary mental system as it provides a general computational architecture. "Production System", comes from the work of the logician Emil

Post who first referred to condition—action rules as productions in the 1940's. Production System architecture, as a standard way of encoding knowledge was originally introduced by Newell and Simon in the late 1960's, in the course their work on human problem solving and was later incorporated by a wide variety of other AI programmers in their expert systems design.

Production systems as defined in the book "Production System models of Learning and Development" edited by David Klahr, Pat Langley and Robert Neches (1987) are a class of computer simulation models that are stated in terms of condition action rules, that make strong assumptions about the nature of the cognitive architecture. Production system models have been viewed in two ways: The first framework treats production system as a formal notation for expressing models. Viewed in this way, it is the content of the model rather than the form of their expression or the interpretation scheme, that is the object of interest. Other formalisms for expressing the same content are possible (e.g. scripts, List programs and flow charts).

In contrast, the second view treats the interpreter of production system as highly specific theory about the architecture of the human information processing system. This view, originally put forward by Newell (1967) and most extensively applied by Anderson (1983) asserts that humans actually employ the functional equivalent of productions in reasoning, understanding language and other intelligent behaviour.

Mitchell Waldrop (1988) states, that, the idea behind the production rules is to encode each bit of knowledge as a condition-action rule of the form, "If this is the case, then do that".

According to Earl Hunt, 1989, in production system programming, there is a privileged symbol structure representing the "current state" of computation and a set of rules (productions) of the form "If (pattern) then take (action)".

Features of a Production System

Neches, Langley and Klahr (1987) describe the basic structure of production system programs. According to them, a production system consists of two interacting data structures, connected through a simple processing cycle. (i) A working memory consisting of a collection of symbolic data items called working memory elements. (ii) A production memory consisting of condition/action rules called productions, whose conditions describe configurations of elements that might appear in working memory and whose actions specify modifications to the content of working memory.

Production memory and working memory are related through the recognize-act cycle consisting of three distinct stages

(a) **The match process,** which finds productions whose conditions match the current state of working memory in different ways and each such mapping is called an instantiation.

(b) **The conflict resolution process,** which selects one or more of the instantiated productions for applications.

(c) **The act process,** which applies the instantiated actions of the selected rules, thus modifying the contents of working memory.

The sequence of matching production rules, performing conflict resolution, and then firing a production is referred to as cycle.

According to Patrick, Henry, Winston (1977) much problem - solving knowledge can be packaged up in the form of little quanta called productions. A production is a rule consisting of a situation recognition part and an action part. When productions are used in deductive systems, the situations that trigger productions are specified Combination of facts.

These authors have represented productions in a form which defines a tree of conclusions called an AND/OR tree which reaches from base facts at the bottom through productions to the conclusion at the top. Any collection of production follows from the AND/OR conjunction of the facts specified in the premise recognition part. A conclusion reached by more than one production is said to the OR or disjunction of those productions. (Fig. taken from Patrick, Henry and Winston, 1977).

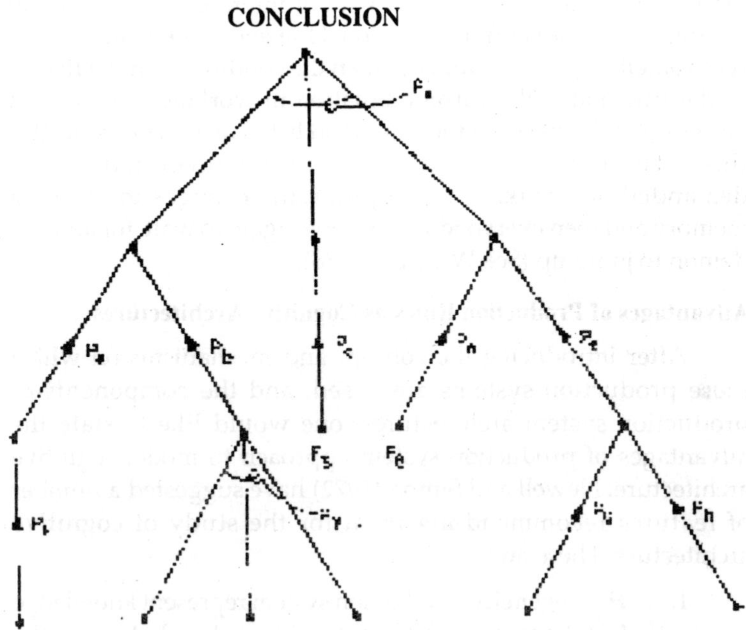

Fig.1.2 A collection of productions defines a tree of conclusions.

Anderson (1993) in his book Rules of the Mind' has outlined the critical features of the Production rules

1. Each production Rule is thought as a modular piece of knowledge, in that it represents a well—defined step of cognition.

2. Complex cognitive processes are achieved by stringing together a sequence of such rules by setting of goals and other writing to working memory, and by reading from working memory.

3. Essential to Production rules are their condition-action asymmetry, which is reflected in many asymmetries of human behaviour.

4. They are abstract and can apply in multiple situations.

H. Mitchell (1988), has likened the production system to a society of little demons-the condition-action rules. These demons spend most of their time in quite contemplation of something called

"Working memory", which is a kind of internal blackboard that records date about current situation. However, when one of them sees something it likes - that is, when the conditions on the IF side of the rule match the current situation in working memory - it jumps up and strikes out the command listed on its Then side "Do this". The programme obeys taking whatever actions are demanded and making the appropriate, changes to working memory and then everyone settles down again to wait. for another demon to jump up (See Waldrop, 1988).

Advantages of Production Rules as Cognitive Architectures

After introducing the concept and mechanisms on which these production systems are based, and the components of production system architectures, one would like to state the advantages of production system approach to model cognitive architecture. Newell and Simon (1972) have suggested a number of features recommend-ing them for the study of cognitive architecture. These are:

1. **Homogeneity:** Production system represent knowledge in a homogenous format, with each rule having the same basic structure and carrying approximately the same amount of information.
2. **Independence:** Production rules are relatively independent of each other making it easy to insert new rules or remove old ones.
3. **Parallel/serial nature:** Production systems combine the notion of a parallel recognition process with a serial application process, both features characteristics of human cognition.
4. **Stimulus-response flavor:** Production systems inherit many of the benefits of stimulus response theory but few of the limitations, since the notions of stimuli and response have been extended to include internal symbbl structures.
5. **Goal-driven behaviour:** Production systems can also be used to model the goal driven character of much human behaviour.

6. **Modeling Memory:** The production system framework offers a viable model of long term memory and its relation to short-term memory since matching and conflict resolution process embody principles of retrieval and focus of attention.

Anderson has also stated certain features of production system which support the use of production system as models for human cognition. One such feature is the flexibility of the production systems. Since production systems could be proposed to account for almost any behaviour human or non-human, production systems have not only been used as psychological systems but there have been attempts to use them as programn~ing formalisms in Artificial Intelligence (Shortliffe and Buchanan, 1975, Davis & King, 1975).

Production systems also have a quality referred to as data driven by Anderson, because each production makes reference to a data base common to all productions and no production makes reference directly to other productions. Production systems are hiqhly modular models and are useful for modeling human behaviour.

Production systems also have an advantage of making extensive use of variables and they can state knowledge in a more general format. Production systems have also some advantages over the stimulus Response Theory. Firstly, it is easy to easy to get a production system to respond to the specific relations among elements but difficult to get a stimulus—response theory to do so. Secondly, an S-R system has no memory for its past beyond memory for its last response. In contrast, production systems can have auxiliary storage medium (short—term memory, chunk structure and productions associative network).(See Anderson, 1983; Klahr et. al. 1987).

History of Production Rules

Although they have their roots in the formalisms of computer science and mathematics, their history can be traced back, as mentioned before, to the proposals of Post (1943). Production system as originally proposed by Post consisted of a set of rules called production for rewriting strings of symbols and a specification of some initial strings called axioms. An example of Post simple production system would be :

Axioms a, b, aa, bb

Production P_1 \$ - a \$ b

P_2 \$ - b \$ b

The relevance of production systems to psychology began with Newell's work at Carnegie-Mellon in the sixties and Waterman's later dissertation Work (1970) at Stanford. Right from the start, according to Anderson, they had ambiguous status being in part programming languages for computer science and in part psychological theories. In Psychology their initial use was to provide theoretical accounts of human performance on a variety of tasks ranging from adults behaviour on various puzzles (Newell & Simon, 1972) to children's responses to class—inclusibn questions (Klahr & Wallace 1973, 1976) & learning (Anderson, Kline & Beasley, 1978; Anzai & Simon, 1979; Langley, Neches, Neves & Anzai 1989).

Research in production systems has continued since the day. The research on the use of productions as signifying cognitive architecture would be reviewed later in the chapter.

The framework of production systems has initiated a number of theories which have been called by Lenat & Harris (1978) "Neoclassical" architecture. Newell's (1980) theories and ideas are based on this approach. Other production systems including ACT theory of Anderson is also a variations in the Neo Classical architecture. The Neoclassical system emphasizes simplicity. It consists of a single uniform working memory, simple rules of conflict resolution. By simple structuring the full space of productions the Neoclassical system makes it easier to define learning mechanism capable of producing the required productions. The Neoclassical system also emphasizes modular productions, in which each production is independent of others which means that production learning can proceed one production at a time without concern for interactions among the productions in a set. (See Anderson, 1983).

Different Production Systems

Over the years multiple production systems have been proposed. R. Neches, P. Langley & D. Klahr (1987) have summarized the evolutionary process of production system architecture in a diagram. (See Neches et. al. 1987).

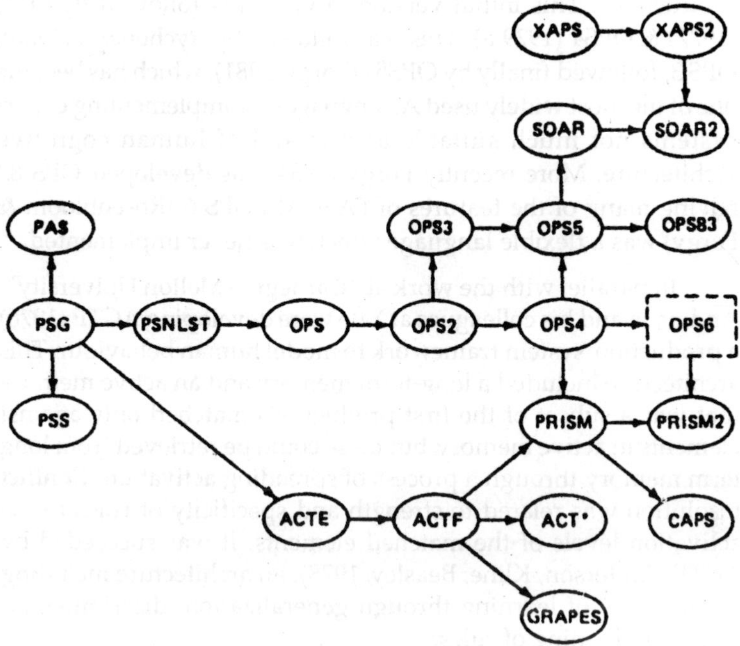

Fig. 1.3 Development of production system architecture Programming

The first widely used production system programming, according to this diagram, was PSG (Newell & Mc'Dermott, 1975) Many of the early production system models were implemented in PSG including Newell's (1973) model of the Steinberg phenomenon & Klahr & Wallace's (1976) developmental stage models. Other early production system language was Waterman's PAS & Ohlsson (1979) P55.

Rychener's PSNLST (1976) emphasized recency as a method of conflict resolution & dynamically recorded productions according to the number of times they have be.en placed pn the candidate match list and thus had number of novel features. Forgy & McDermott (1976) developed the first version of OPS to be used by Allen Newell at Carnegie-Mellon University. The most important feature of OPS was its pattern matcher, which allowed it to compute efficiently the matched instantiations of all productions. This initial version of OPS was followed by 0P52 (1977) & OPS4 (1979 a). This was followed by Rychener's (1980), OPS 3, followed finally by OPS5~(Forgy, 1981), which has become one of the most widely used Al languages for implementing expert systems not much suitable as a model of human cognitive architecture. More recently Forgy (1984) has developed OPS 83 having many of the features of PASCAL. OPS 6 (Rosenbloom & Forgy) was a flexible language which was never implemented.

In parallel with the work at "Carnegie - Mellon University", Anderson and his colleagues at Yale were developing ACTE (1976) a production-system framework to model human behaviour. This architecture included a long-term memory and an active memory that was a subset of the first productions matched only against elements in active memory, but these could be retrieved from long term memory through a process of spreading activation. Conflict resolution was related to strength and specificity of rules to the activation levels of the matched elements. It was succeeded by ACTF (Anderson, Kline, Beasley, 1978), an architecture including mechanisms of learning through generalization, discrimination and strengthening of rules.

Anderson developed two architectures, ACTG & ACTH in 1978, which existed only in transitory form. These were followed by GRAPES (Sauers and Farrell, 1982), a production system language that placed goals in special memory. Anderson (1983) developed ACT with the GRAPES effort which was the final installation in the ACT series of architectures. Langley & Neches (1981) developed PRISM which incorporated features of OPS 4, ACTF etc. Based on PRISM code Thibadeau (1982) developed CAPS an activation-based architecture.

PRISM 2 (Langley, Ohlsson, Thibadeau & Walter, 1984) was developed to remove the limitations faced by PRISM. XAP5 (1979) AND XAPS2 architectures were developed by Rosenbloom (1979) based on his interest in motor behavior. Laird (1983) developed

SOAR, an architecture that combined the production system framework, with Newell's (1980) problem space hypothesis. Finally SOAR was followed by SOAR 2 an architecture developed by Laird, Rosenbloom & Newell (1984), which combined SOAR with Chunking abilities of XAPS2.

These were the frameworks on which many architectures were based.

The ACT Production System

In 1976 Anderson developed the ACTE production system followed by ACTF. Both systems were developed as simulation programs. ACT was developed to integrate the performance subtheories with the learning subtheories and was a final step in the scientific progress.

The general framework for the ACT production system, identifying the major structural components and their interlinking processes is shown in Fig. 1.4 (taken from Anderson, 1983). An ACT production system consists three memories Working, declarative and production. **Working memory,** as mentioned earlier, contains the information that the system can currently access, consisting of information retrieved from long term declarative memory as well as temporary structures deposited by encoding processes and the action of productions.

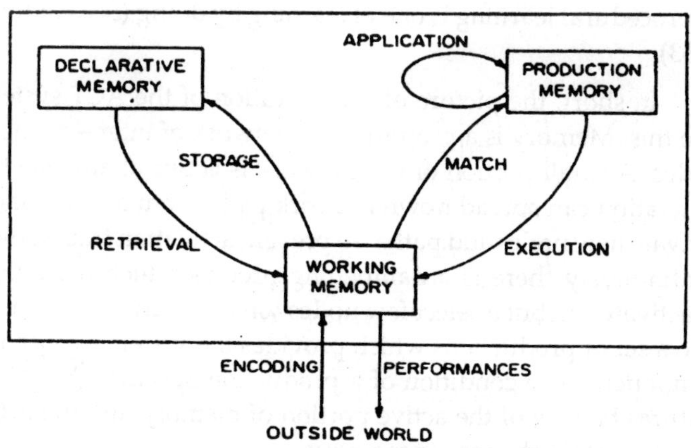

Fig. 1.4 An ACT production system

Basically, the working memory in the ACT production system refers to declarative knowledge permanent or temporary, that is in an active state. The ACT model makes a fundamental distinction between Procedural and declarative knowledge—between knowing how and knowing that. Procedural knowledge is represented in terms of productions and declarative knowledge is represented in terms of a propositional network. This is contrasted to Newell and Sirnonts suggestion that all knowledge procedural and declarative is represented in terms of productions. As shown in the figure, encoding processes deposit information about the outside world into the working memory; **performance** processes coiivert commands in working memory into behaviour. The **storage** process can create permanent records in declarative memory of the contents of working memory and can increase the strength of existing records in declarative memory. The **retrieval** process retrieves information from declarative memory. In the **match** process, data in working memory are put into correspondence with the conditions of productions. The **execution** process deposits the actions of matched productions into working memory. The whole process of **production matching** followed by execution is referred to as production **application**. The arrow called application, cycling back in to the production memory box reflects that new productions are learned from studying the history of application of existing productions. Thus Anderson's ACT theory of procedural learning is one of learning by doing (See Anderson, 1983).

In short, the picture of the operation of the ACT system is like this. Memory is a propositional network of inter—connected nodes. A small portion of this network is active at any one time. Activation can spread down network paths from active nodes to activate new nodes and paths. To prevent activation from growing continuously there is a dampening process which periodically deactivates all but a select few nodes (on the Active List). There is also a set of productions which provides the system's procedural component. The condition of a production specifies that certain features be true of the active portion of memory and the actions specify certain changes to memory.

Anderson, faced the problem of implementation with his earlier ACT theory that led to the various revisions and finally the mechanisms in ACT were tuned and slightly changed in ACT-R (See Anderson, 1993) to yield adaptive processing.

Other Cognitive Architectures

Production systems are not unique as cognitive architectures. To go back to an earlier era, Hullian theory (Hull, 1951) would constitute a cognitive architecture. The architecture proposed by Anderson, Newell & Simon and others is an architecture based on production systems. The same generality and universality in modeling human cognition can also be achieved by some other different architectures. The most common alternative to production systems are the various schema architectures (Bobrow & Winograd, 1977, Minsky, 1975, Rumelhart & Ortony, 1976, Schank & Abelson, 1977).

The two major components of schema framework are working memory and schema memory. The major control cycle of this system involved matching schemata to the contents of working memory. Thus, recognition is the basic force. Information enters working memory from the environment but also by the action of schemata specifically, if a schema is partially matched by the information in working memory, it will create further information to complete the match. Schemata are organized hierarchically according to a part structure. In matching the whole schema it may be necessary to invoke matching the part schema and matching the part schema may invoke matching the whole.

The Action related to schema theories, as proposed by Abelson (1981), Rumelhart and Ortony (1976), is that, in matching a schema to a situation and in adding pieces, one can add instructions to act.

The first major problem of schema theory is that it blurs the procedural-declarative distinction and leaves unexplained all the contrasts between procedural and declarative knowledge. It also leaves unexplained the automatization phenomena. A second major problem with schema (Anderson 1976) is that the units of knowledge tend to be too large, thus forcing the system into modes of behavior that are too limited. A production system, having smaller units permits richer possibility for recombination to explain flexibility in human intelligence.

Popular, more recent alternatives to production system architectures are the various connectionist theories. The idea behind this connectionist modeling is to derive a pattern recognition system from mathematical idealizations of networks of Neuron—like elements. The behavior of the network, as a whole, is a function of the initial state of activation of the units and of the weights on its connections, which serves as its only form of memory. There is an attempt to propose connectionism as providing an account of the neural (or 'abstract neurological') structures in which classical cognitive architecture is implemented. (Fodor & Pylyshyn, 1988). But till further developments in the connectionist models take place and till various frameworks formulate theories about the working of human mind, till then, production rules constitute a suitable framework for under—standing human cognition. The Psychological reality of these rules has been acknowledged by various researchers. Thus J.A. Anderson & Hinton (1981) acknowledged that "well learned and regular interactions between patterns of activity can be captured as explicit rules governing manipulation of abstract symbols" and Smolensky (1986) recognized that "novices are described by productions with simple conditions and actions and experts are described by complex conditions and actions." (See Anderson, 1993).

Goodman, Rodney M., Higgins, Charles M., Miller, John W. and Smythe, Padhraic (1992) proposed a network architecture that combines a rule—based approach with that of the neural network paradigm. A model of the domain knowledge is a set of probabilistic conjunctive rules between discrete input evidence variables and output class variables. These are then mapped on the weights and nodes of a feed forward neural network resulting in a directly specified architecture.

In summary, the argument for the psychological reality of production rules according to Anderson (1993), involves two layers of evidence; One is the manifest appropriateness of rules in describing many aspects of skilled behavior. The second is the ability to predict the details of that behavior under a production-rule description.

Review of the Related Studies

History of Research on Production Systems

The early production system models were not programmed for the computer and required "hand—simulation". The first running production system was that of Waterman's (1970) poker playing program. This was as a model for human learning.

Following Newell and Simon (1972) pioneering work, the literature exhibits a serious interest in study of various cognitive phenomena employing production system approach. Newell's (1972) first application focused on stimulus encoding and the second (Newell, 1973) modeled performance on the Sternberg memory-scanning paradigms.

A few years later Waterman (1975) gave new results with adaptive production systems. One of these systems implemented EPAM like discrimination networks as production rules and another focused on sequence extrapolation tasks. One year later, Rychener (1976) completed a thesis in which he reimplemented a variety of well—known AI systems as production systems and demonstrated that production system framework was a powerful representational scheme and was useful for modeling intelligence.

Anderson, Kline and Lewis (1977) used production systems to model the complexities of natural language under standing, and Anderson (1976) applied them to a variety of other information processing tasks. Thibadeau, Just and Carpenter (1982) went even further showing how production system models could account for reaction time phenomena in reading tasks. Finally, Ohlsson (1980 b) used the production system framework to model detailed verbal protocols on the transitive reasoning tasks. The researches mentioned above were dealing with the mechanisms of learning. Production systems framework was also used to model the various stages of cognitive development. Klahr and Wallace (1973, 1976) carried out the earliest work of this type when they constructed stage models of behaviour on a variety of Piagetian tasks including class inclusion and conservation of quantity. The basic approach involved modeling behaviour at different stages in terms of production system programs that differed by only one or a few rules.

Baylor, Gascon, Lemoyne and Pother (1973) extended this approach to Piagetian length and weight seriation tasks, and young (1976) carried out an even more detailed analysis of length seriation in his thesis research. Klahr and Siegler (1978) developed similar production-system stage models for Piaget's balance scale task, combining this with detailed empirical studies of children's behaviour on the task, Larkin (1981) used production-system framework to model adult expert-novice differences in physics problem solving and ohlsson (1980 a) modeled similar differences in ability of his transitive reasoning tasks.

Shortly, thereafter, production system models became an active research area. Anzai (1978) reported a model of human learning on the Tower of Hanoi puzzle and Neves (1978) proposed a model of algebra learning. Langley (1978) developed an adaptive production system for concept attainment, sequence extrapolation and simple empirical discovery and McDermott (1979) described a production system approach to reasoning by analogy.

Production System Architecture: Learning

Investigators have used production systems to understand various learning tasks. The most commonly studied task was' "learning from examples" in which imprqvement consists of increasing one's ability to correctly predict exemplors and non exemplors of the concept (See Winston, 1975, Hayes-Roth and Mc Dermott 1978, Anderson and Kline (l979), Michalski, Utgoff and Banerji 1983) . Very few researchers have attempted to model human learning in this domain (Anzai, 1978, Ohlsson, 1983).

The speed up' process as an account for learning have been studied by Lewis (1978), Neches (1981) and Neves and Anderson (1981). Laird, Rosenbloom and Newell (1984) outlined a production theory that accounted for "speed up" and "reduce search".

The task of language acquisition in the form of grammar learning has been studied by Hedrick (1976), Berwick (1979),

Anderson (1981) and Langley (1982). The goal of these studies was to generate rules for mapping sentences onto their meanings or meanings onto grammatical sentences.

Studies have also illustrated the side effects of the learning process. Neves and Anderson (1981) have shown a phenomena **Einstelling** which arises naturally from their composition model of speed up and is related to lack of flexibility, in problem solving behaviour.

Production System: Learning Mechanisms

In the production system architecture learning mechanism or recognize act cycle or the change of behaviour is an outcome of

1. The process of matching productions
2. The process of conflict resolution and
3. The process of applying productions.

Different mechanisms have been proposed in terms of the manner in which they affect the recognize act cycle of the production systems. Waterman (1970, 1975) in his study, took the approach of adding new rules above those productions they were intended to mask (since rules were matched in linear order) Forgy (1979b) presented an efficient method for computing all matched instations.

Another mechanism of learning in the form of modifying the conditions of existing rules or to construct variants on existing rules with slightly different condition sides was studied by Anderson, Kline and Beasley (1978) calling the mechanism of modifying rules as 'generalization' and 'discrimination'.

These techniques of Rule Modification have been used in programs modeling behaviour on concept acquisition experiments (Anderson and Kline, 1979), language comprehension and production at various age levels (Langley 1982, Anderson 1981) Geometry theorem proving (Anderson, Greeno, Kline and Neves, 1981) and various puzzle-solving tasks (Langley, 1982).

Lewis (1978) studied another mechanism called Chunking in which two or more rules combine into a new rule with conditions and actions of component rules accounting for speed up as a result of practice.

Any production systems model of learning must take into account, according to R. Neches, P. Langley and D. Klahr,, the parameters used during conflict resolution. The mechanisms that have been proposed that leads to rules with new conditions and actions take the form of composition, to account for speed up as a result of practice (Lewis, 1978). This method combines two or more rules into a new rule with conditions and actions of component rules. This was one form of chunking.

Another mechanism proposed for creating new rules called proceduralization was studied by Neves and Anderson (1981) and applied to transitive reasoning tasks by Qhlsson. This method leads to speed up effects and automatization.

Evidence, coming from studies that have tried to characterize difference between expert and novice solution methods for algebra expression (Lewis, 1981) , and from analysis of the procedures employed by a mental calculator (Hunter, 1968) have led Neves and Anderson (1981) to propose a knowledge compilation model, which is another mechanism of learning.

Other studies on expert/novice differences in Physics problem solving (Simon and Simon, 1978; Larkin 1981) have also shown that composition, generalization and discrimination are not sufficient to account for all learning. Studies by Neches (1981 b) and Anzai and Simon (1979) have pointed out that learning appears to involve reasoning on the basis of knowledge about the structures of procedures, in general, and the semantics of a given procedure, in particular, involving both general and domain— specific knowledge about procedures.

Production System: Skill Acquisition

John R. Anderson (1987) in his article on Skill Acquisition' has stated, that, people solve problems in new domains by applying weak problem - solving procedures to declarative knowledge they have about this domain. From these initial problem solutions, productions rules are compiled that are specific to that domain and that use of knowledge. Thus, he has emphasized the critical role of the production rule, a computational improvement over the stimulus — response bond, in organizing the research on acquisition of cognitive skills.

Anderson and Reiser (1985), studied how productions are combined to solve a problem, and how domain-specific productions are acquired from domain—general productions. They observed 38 subjects solve the problem of writing functions in LISP. They concluded that problem solving by analogy, as shown by their subjects, can be well modeled by a production system with a hierarchical goal structure.

Research on the acquisition of ~cognitive skills, therefore has received a great deal of attention within the Artificial Intelligence literature (J.R. Anderson, 1981, 1982, 1983; Brown and Van Lehn 1980; Carbonell 1983; Chi, Glaser and Farr, 1988; Kieras and Bovair 1986; Laird, Rosenbloom and Newell 1984; Langley, 1982; Larkin, Mc Dermott, Simon and Simon 1980; Lesgold 1984; Newell and Rosenbloom 1981 and Van Lehn 1983).

Before the development of Act theory, there was little evidence to support acquisition of skills over long time courses. But Anderson in his research tried to study complex mathematical and technical skills such as geometry, programming and text editing etc. His most ambitions line of research has been into domain—specific productions. Anderson (1982) in the study of geometry proof generalization also studied knowledge compilation process. He concludes that, on an average of more than 100 rules used by the LISP tutor, the Second time a rule is used the number of errors and time both drop less than half.

Knowledge compilation process emphasizes the goal structure because it indicates which steps of the original solution belong together J.R. Anderson (1982) predicted a number of empirical phenomena by the knowledge compilation process. These include :

(a) The dramatic one trial speed up in performance of a new rule.

(b) The concomitant drop out of verbalization, since the knowledge is now encoded procedurally rather than declaratively.

(c) The disappearance of set size effects with practice (Schneider and Shiffrin, 1977).

The ACT theory predicts that there will be positive transfer between skills to the extent that the two skills involve the same production. Singley and Anderson (1985) used text editing as a task to analyze the production rule prediction of transfer. There already existed production□ system models of this task (Card, Moran and Newell, 1983; Kieras and Polson, 1985) though they were not ACT production systems.

Effects of knowledge compilation Knowledge compilation, the basic learning mechanism of ACT, leads to a lot of implications, for example, it implies that frequently occurring combinations of operations should gain an advantage over less frequently co-occuring combinations of the same operations. McKendree and Anderson studied this prediction. They hypothesized that knowledge compilation process predicts a speed up advantage in evaluating high, frequency combinations because of two factors:

(a) The compiled productions for the high frequency combinations are likely to be learned sooner and

(b) Once learned they will acquire strength more rapidly because of their greater frequency.

Studying the subjects ability to evaluate various combinations of LISP expressions they got results supporting the hypotheses.

However, according to Anderson, knowledge compilation often derives productions from declarative knowledge that can be used only in certain ways. Thus, in many situations the ACT theory does not predict transfer between different uses of the same knowledge. Neves and Anderson (1981) compared subjects' ability to generate a proof in a logic like system with their ability to give the reasons that justified the statements of a worked out proof. They found evidence, that, 10 days of practice at giving a reason had no significant positive transfer to proof generation.

McKendree and Anderson studied the transfer in their study of LISP evaluation skills. They found that productions that solved the evaluation problems and productions that solved the generation problem did not overlap, although these productions were based on the same abstract declarative knowledge. This implies basically the same knowledge in different form. They tried to study whether massive practice on evaluation would generalize to generation. Their experiment showed that there are qualitative changes with practice in a skill and it is not just a matter of everything becoming informally better. The ACT theory was supported in the sense, that the difference in form is significant and there will not be transfer between the two forms.

Singley and Anderson (1985) tested the qualitative changes implied by proceduralization - i.e., content based interference should disappear when the knowledge is proceduralized. The results were consistent with the view.

Working memory failures J.R. Anderson and Jeffries (1985) and Jeffries (1985) studied the working memory failures as the major source of errors made by 100 students in introductory LISP classes. He found that increasing the complexity of one part of the problem increased errors in another part, suggesting that capacity requirements to represent one part overflowed and had an impact on the representation of another part. The errors were also found to be nonsystgematic.

Jeffries et al. (1981) found that memory capacity was a major difference separating beginning programmers from experienced programmers. Chase and Ericsson (1982) found that storage of domain information in long—term memory became so reliable that long—term memory developed into an effective extension of short term memory. As a consequence of working memory failure, the answer will be missing some information. The errors resulting from working memory overload have been studied J.R. Anderson and Jeffries (1985), Katz and Anderson (1985) and Norman (1981).

Their results were consistent with the hypothesis that errors increase with working load.

M.W. Lewis and Anderson (1985) performed an experiment to study the effect of Immediate Feedback and its interaction with compilation and working memory. They found that subjects performed considerably better, in terms of number of correct moves, when given immediate feedback. Other researchers (R.C. Anderson, Kulhavy, Andre, 1972) found that the type of feedback was critical to determine its effectiveness.

Further Implications for Instructions: Intelligent Tutoring

Various studies have focused on the value of instruction and the types of instructions. Pirolli and Anderson (1984) developed an ACT production system model of recrusive programming.

The results showed that students given how—to information took 57 minutes whereas students given the how-it—works information look 95 mm thus confirming the effectiveness of how—to instructions.

J.R. Anderson and Reiser (1985) have also studied the importance of LISP tutors as compared to students solving the problems on their own. The students scored better and took less time when tutored to solve recrusion section of a paper and pencil final exam.

Work on intelligent tutoring according to Anderson (1993) refers to efforts to create computer—based system for instruction using artificial intelligence approaches. His approach to development of intelligent tutors was called the model-tracing approach (Anderson, Boyle, Corbett and Lewis, 1990). It involves developing a cognitive model of the skill that should be learned (e.g. doing proofs in geometry or writing computer programs in the language of LISP). Anderson's model takes the form of a set of production rules that can solve the class of problems the student is being asked to solve in the same way that the student should solve the problems. The researchers assumed that the student is taking an overall means-ends approach and learning involves acquiring production rules that encode operators to use within this problem-solving organization. The tutor in the study tries to interpret the student's problem-solving in terms of the firing of a set of production rules in its cognitive model. They also developed methods for actually diagnosing the student's behavior and attributing segments of the problem-solving behavior to the operation of specific production rules. The results have pointed out to students performing one standard deviation better than control classrooms (if given the same amount of time on task).

Thus Anderson, in his book, "Rules of the Mind" has identified some general factors that determine how well subjects perform within the tutor. In the case of LISP, these factors turn out to be a) the speed with which subjects acquire new rules and b) the degree to which they retain old rules. In case of geometry, these factors are a) the success students have with algebraic rules and b) the success they have with rules that involve spatial relations.

He concluded that the production rule is serving much of the same function that had been assigned to the stimulus-response bond in past theories. The skill appears to be nothing more than a sum of these rules. Each rule is learned independently and individual differences are reflected in the learning of these rules and not the performance of these rules once acquired.

Inductive Learning Finally the ACT learning mechanisms also include inductive learning mechanisms of generalization and discrimination. In the ACT theory, these processes are regarded as automatic processes not subject to strategic influences and not open to conscious inspection. Reber (1976) in his study on unconscious learning supported this viewpoint.

However, there is evidence which questions this automaticity. First, Elio and Anderson (1984), Kline (1A83) in their experiments have found that the generalizations people form from their experience are subject to strategic control. Second M.W. Lewis and Anderson (1985) in their experiment found that subjects were able to restrict the application of a problem—solving operator (i.e., discriminate a production) only if they could consciously formulate the discrimination rule. Dulany, Carlson and Dewey (1984), have found that even in Reber's unconscious learning situation, subjects had conscious—access to low-level rules that help them classify the examples.

Thus, Anderson (1986) has concluded that the inductive process of generalization and discrimination are things that can be implemented by a set of problem-solving productions. Knowledge compilation can convert these inductive problems solving episodes into productions that generalize beyond the current problem.

Production System Architecture to Study Specific Skills/Problems

The study of mathematical thinking and performance became an important issue with the advent of Cognitive Science. Concern has been shown in improving the mathematics education because of failure children face in learning mathematics leading to mathematics phobia. Teaching Mathematical procedures does not only involve the lesson in technical skills. Resnick and Omanson, have suggested that more general mathematical principles underlie the performance of procedures. The introduction of the production system as a framework in the study of arithmetic learning (Newell and Simon, 1972) has enabled researchers to single out, from among detailed subskills, those that are prerequisites for the entire skill.

Riley and Greeno (1980) has studies counting of N objects using simplified production systems. The results showed that counting is not merely a verbal act as suggested by Piaget (1952). It involves two independent progressions, that have to be coordinated: the progression in the list of number words and the progression of the tagged (marked) objects that are counted. The production system formalization also revealed the need to mark the right way of beginning as well as ending the process. These subprocesses are executed automatically by grown—ups who are experts in counting; but may cause some difficulties for the naive learner and take some time to master.

The model of counting presented by Riley and Greeno (1980) was a computer model. Other studies have empirically tested various counting skills like ability to recite an ordered string of words or the ability to make a one—to—one correspondence between the number words and the tagged objects (Gelman & Gallistel 1987; Gelman & Neck, 1983). These studies illustrated that even the partial recognition and analysis of the subskills underlying procedural learning can be used as powerful tools in instructional setting.

Siegler and Shrager (1983), in describing changes occuring due to child's development, suggested a strategy choice that is problem dependent for every individual, depending on the distribution of associative strengths that an individual has developed through prior experience, including the various problems and the solution efforts the individual has generated. Pearla Nesher (1986) has suggested that the process of constructing and lumping subprocedures for counting into one chunk serves later as the control and backing system for the declarative knowledge. Thus, in learning mathematics sufficient amount of propositional knowledge of basic arithmetic facts has to be tied to the procedural knowledge as a control in performing these tasks.

Mary Vakali (1984-85), has studied Arithmeticword problems as solved by the 9 year olds which involves mental arithmetic. The results implied that the strategy used by the subjects in solving mathematics word problems involves applying procedural as well as declarative knowledge, that is, by using rules for carrying, borrowing and keeping track (procedural) along with fact retrieval of sums & differences (declarative).

The problem, Tower of Hanoi, has been studied by many people using the production system, approach (See Newell and Simon, 1972; Simon, 1975; Karat, 1982; Anzai and Simon, 1972). Kolovsky, J.R. Hayes and H.A. Simon (1985) analyzed the causes for large differences in difficulties of various isomorphic versions of the Tower of Hanoi problem. They concluded that,

(i) The problem rules are a major source of problem difficulty and differences in difficulty.

(ii) Rule compatibility is a major influence on transfer of training.

(iii) Rules consistent with real world knowledge aid problem solving by reducing the memory load imposed by the rules.

(iv) Intensive training in the rules, even in isolation from any problem setting or knowledge significantly decreases the difficulty of the problems.

(v) Spatial or positional information is somewhat privileged.

(vi) Providing a good external representation aid problem solving and removing information from the external representation hinders problem solving.

Their analysis sets forth a view that the problem solver has a limited amount of processing capacity that is easily overloaded by the memory requirements of unfamiliar problems rules. This overload prevents even minimal amounts of necessary planning from occuring. In problems where training and practice are possible, this limitation can be overcome through the automatization of some of the knowledge which will allow planning, learning and generalization to occur. This has been supported by Wason and Shapiro (1971), Wason (1972), and Johnson-Laird etc. (1972). Their work on logic problems showed that errors are sharply reduced by the introduction of problem isomorphs that involve familiar materials instead of unfamiliar problems.

Anazai, Mitsaya, Nakajima and Ura, 1981 developed a production system model containing 31 production to simulate the strategy-learning process for a seriation task. It predicted two different but successful strategies for this problem.

P. Langley (1982, 1983) has also studies concept attainment, strategy learning, first language acquisition (AMBER) and development on a piagetian task using the production system framework, based on theory of discriminative learning that begins with overly general rules and creates variants of these rules with additional conditions when these rules lead to errors. They described SAGE, an adaptive production system in studying, strategy learning using the slide-jump puzzle.

Montare (1992) studied the knowledge one acquires from learning, whether it was procedural or declarations. The design of his study allowed subjects to achieve procedural cognizance without possessing declarative cognizance of that knowledge. On the basis of his results, he concluded, that differential declarative cognizance of equal procedural cognition has been demonstrated. The major theoretical postulate of the present study is that the observed differences in declarative cognizance are based on different learning processes.

Studies Comparing Visually Impaired and Sighted

Information is essential for any system to work. Without the ability to receive, process and store information, there would be little one could do effectively. Human development requires exposure to information and learning to process this material meaningfully. Most of the information which forms the declarative component has been achieved by the multiple sensory systems, that have evolved to perceive the same world. The current evidence suggests that multiple neural centres extract different but overlapping information from the visual signals (Anderson 1983). Mind, therefore, also evolves multiple overlapping systems to optimize various aspect of mental process ing, supporting the role of senses in achieving information, Bushnell (1981) considers the senses as active instruments which seek and explore, providing performing knowledge before conscious knowledge. Intersensory behaviors seem to be supported by some sort of conceptual awareness of sensory inputs. When this cross modal knowledge, developing during the early days is complete, there is differentiation in addition to integration, and according to Bushnell (1981) "the ontogeny of intermodal relations is not a simple, unitary process but is instead, a many faceted one, the development of which is gradual, complex and interdependent with expertness and with developments."

Abravanel (1981) discussed integration of information from the eyes and the hands and concluded that perceptual exploration that is either visual or haptic gives common characteristics. There is improvement with age related to general development in perceptions and knowledge across all sensory systems.

Millar (1981) concluded that sense modalities are neither separate nor unitary. They are complementary and convergent.

The loss of vision is regarded to be the most damaging of any sensory loss. When the visual system is impaired or completely non—functional, reliance on the sensory systems increases in direct proportion to the degree of visual impairment. Just how it affects the transfer of and integration of information for perceptual and cognitive networks or in Anderson's words for propositional network is not fully understood. According to Millar (1981) absence of active interaction is more detrimental than deprivation of vision in constructing sensory motor schema.

Although vision, touch and movement all contribute to sensory integration, each emphasizes different aspects of information about the world. According to Anater (1980) loss of vision requires a shift to auditory and haptic systems which may provide contradictory information when individuals are trying to rely on stored visual images. In his experiment, he concluded that haptic information did not have to be converted to an auditory format. Thus it can be said that coding process may be unique to each person. With the loss of sight, perceptions may be different because they are based on nonvisual information intake which is likely to affect the integrating process.

Concepts are achieved through a process of associating numerous perceptions developed from all sensory data, and from the processed information, formulating ideas about the world. Concepts may range from functional to abstract depending on the quantity and quality of information upon which the ideas are based. Thus, the sensory loss, in the form of vision loss, would also affect the temporal strings, spatial images and abstract propositions. In fact, abstract propositions will have a dominant role if the blind children actively participate in their environment.

Numerous speculations are offered to to possible effect of visual impairment on cognitive development and functioning but no definite conclusions have come forth. Mental images of cognitally visually handicapped persons are likely to be fewer in number and possibly less accurate than those stored by individuals with normal vision. Hall (1981) has concluded that since the referents for imagery are different for blind persons and for some low vision ones the forms of mental images may also differ from those of sighted people.

Several investigators have studied various areas of cognitive functioning, mental imagery and reasoning abilities in the visually impaired children. Rubin (1964) compared abstract functioning among congenitally blind, adventitiously blinded and sighted persons and found that the blind persons performed less well than both the other groups on a series of test of abstractions.

Witkin and his associates (1968) conducted a study on cognitive patterning in congenitally totally blind children and said that to form impressions of objects as discrete and as structured through senses other than vision was possible but much more difficult.

As a group, blind children has less developed articulation than did a matched group of sighted children but the difference was not as great as expected by the researchers. Some blind children showed highly developed abilities to analyze and structure their thinking suggesting that blindness may serve as an "impetus to the development of differentiation."

A study by Witkin and associates, 1971, concluded that lack of vision slows the pace in visual progression in cognitive development from global to articulated but not greatly. Congenitally blind children were equivalent to sighted children in verbal comprehension ability but superior in tasks requiring prolonged auditory attention.

Boldt (1969) presented some interesting views in regard to the way blind pupils develop abstract thought patterns. He concludes that development of concepts in blind children would be understood as a process of progressive dissociation of subject and object, and only towards the end of this dissociation, real conceptualization is attained.

Higgins (1973) in his study of classification in blind children found that they did not exhibit a significant development lag in the attainment of classificatory logic indicating "that the condition of total congenital blindness *per se* is not sufficient to produce a delay in the formation of the intellectual structures underlying classification."

Stephens and Grube (1982) found concrete reasoning to be the same between blind children and a matched group of sighted children but logical thought requiring mental imagery or spatial perspective was decidedly below that of the sighted children of the same age. They found that remediation was successful, in that, the experimental group was superior to the control group on 17 of the 26 variables. The two areas where no improvement was noted were mental imagery and classification.

The majority of studies on cognitive development in blind children find that some concepts are learned at the symbolic level only and that it is difficult to use them in problem-solving situations, concrete reasoning appears to be no different than in sighted individuals, mental images need to formed by direct experience (Hall, 1981; Millar, 1981; Stephens and Grube, 1982). Manyresearchers have also noted that congenitally blind children may conceptualize the world differently from their sighted peers because their lack of vision hampers their integration and organization of sensory information, limits their mobility and obstructs their interaction with object, events and other persons in the environment (Santin and Nesker, Simmons, 1977; Scholl, 1973; wills, 1965).

Davidson (1976), Foulke (1964), Santin and Nesker, Simmons (1977) have concluded sighted children's mental images or concepts of objects, which are based on their visually directed experience of objects, may not match those of blind children which are generated through touch, hearing, smell and taste—sense that provide inconsistent bits of information.

David W. Anderson (1984), studied the mental representation of objects in 10 totally and congenitally blind children, aged 3-9 and a matching group of 10 sighted children, who were asked to describe, first from memory and then through tactual exploration, selected common objects.

The data suggested, that, mental images or concept of objects that blind children develop significantly deviates from those acquired by sighted children through visually guided actions. The authors suggested that blind children develop their mental images or concept of objects from their unique experience and their form of mental representation, rather than, from their knowledge of the language of sighted people. Both the blind and sighted children in the study seem to have constructed concepts of objects based on first hand action oriented experiences.

Sally M. Bailes and Robert M. Lambert (1986) studied using haptic form recognition tasks, the hypothesis, that the adventitiously blind have retained some ability to encode successive information, obtained haptically in terms of a global visual representation while the congenitally blind use a coding system based on successive inputs. The results did not support the above hypothesis. Three main findings were obtained i) normally sighted subjects were both faster and more accurate than the other groups. ii) all groups improved in accuracy of recognition as a function of length of interstimulus interval. iii) sighted subjects tended to report using strategies with a strong verbal component while the blind tended to rely of imagery coding. They concluded the imagery processing of visual information is quick and so for sighted subjects using vision, the segments are quickly encoded into a global representation and can then be transferred to short-term working storage. Imagery manipulation with haptic information may be much slower or more difficult, however, possibly to the extent that, for the blind subjects, the integration of the segment is not completed before the onset of the next segment.

Thus, all subjects improve with the longer delay intervals, as the assembling process becomes more advanced. However, only the sighted using vision progressed to the stage where the information could be verbally labeled in the delays allowed in the study. If the blind were given longer delays it is possible that they would make systematic use of verbal labels and their accuracy would improve to the level of the sighted subjects.

Mark Hollins (1985) also studied the styles of mental imagery in blind adults. It was found that greater the proportion of life for which, each of the blind subject had been without sight, the less was his or her pictorial score, expressed as a proportion of total imagery score. This showed that nature of mental imagery slowly changes following the loss of sight.

Rossana De Beni and Cesare Cornoldi (1988) conducted a series of experiments requiring memorization of single nouns, pairs of nouns or triplets of nouns associated with a cue noun to explore the limitations of representations produced by the absence of visual experience. The found that recall by blind students was impaired when multiple interactive images (with nouns pairs and triplets) are formed. The poorer recall of blind subjects ref lected also loss of order information. Recall was better for both groups with locative noun cues and high-imagery targets. The results suggested that totally congenitally blind people may encounter difficulty in using visual imagery. The more limited experience of the blind may give them a representation of meanings which is more literal less rich and less flexible and consequently less suitable for multiple and unusual connections.

The visually impaired child's representation is different from that of sighted. The sighted can represent information about colour of objects semantically and visually, the blind are limited to semantic representations. Even in the case of representation of tangible objects the blind have to rely on other imagery modalities than visual and semantic representations. These findings are evident in all the studies mentioned above comparing blind and sighted on mental imagery and various cognitive skills. But, Peter W. Shehan and Jan Jilden (1983) on the contrary, have found that congenitally blind perform as well as the sighted on tasks involving information about visual phenomena and images of spatial configurations. The results of their study did show that blind performed more poorly than the sighted in the free recall task in which they showed less clustering than the sighted on "red" words. These results were consistent with the fact that the blind must acquire knowledge about non tangible visual phenomena th.rough instruction and thus would be expected to lag in their acquisition of this knowledge, behind the sighted, who can acquire it directly.

The propositionalist point of view proposed by Anderson (1978) implies a common format for the representation of information in long term memory. The studies mentioned above, specially the ones which study imagery limitations in the visually impaired as compared to sighted, state that, this unitary representation does exist even for the blind but they have limitations because of limitations of experience. The above studies have also shown that these limitations can be overcome by instructions and training.

Concluding, it becomes evident from the literature that production system architecture is a suitable framework for studying cognitive architecture in humanbeings, for many environmental situations like solving puzzles, acquiring specific skills and building general models for learning various tasks. Not much work has been carried out employing this approach in the study of cognitive architecture of the visually impaired. The studies mentioned in this chapter have compared blind and sighted children on various Cognitive processes and cognitive development and have outlined specific theories related to various cognitive functions.

2

Problem and Objectives

Problem

The appropriateness of the production system framework has already been discussed. Studies have shown that production rule is a computational improvement over the Stimulus Response Bond in research on Problem Solving (Anderson, 1990). It has been shown to be prone to learning and training (Anderson, 1990, Neches, Langley and Klahr, 1987).

In recent years, attention to matters like learning, transition mechanisms, cognitive skills and interventions which fostered the acquisition of knowledge and cognitive skills has been increasing with the advent of Cognitive Science. Production system models, are structures that combine both what we know and how we must act and permit intelligent actions. They have been shown to be ideal frameworks for simulating human performances in simple tasks. According to Young (1979) production systems are also very well suited to approach human behavior involving a choice on the basis of a fixed amount of task—specification information collected over the years. They are clear and powerful ways of representing symbol processing. The motivations for production system architecture have been many. In being well structured, they contrast with theoretical formalisms such as neural models (McClelland and Rumelhart, 1986; Rumelhart and McClelland, 1986). This good structuring helps guarantee that the behavior produced by learning production rules will be coherent. It is possible to delete or add production rules individually. This independence of production rules makes it possible to define an incremental learning system that grows one production rule at a time and does not involve wholesale changes to the cognitive procedures (Anderson, 1987).

The cognitive analysis of performance with the help of production rules has made it possible to reveal outcomes of learning and measure developing expertise. This knowledge is useful in theorizing about how these abilities are learned and in instructional designs that foster learning. Instructional investigations by cognitive scientists have led to the designing of computer tutors. Studies of expert-novice differences with the help of production-system architecture have contributed to developing competence in the area of knowledge.

Conceptually, the study concern was to examine the features of cognitive architecture in the visually Impaired and in order to bring out the distinctive features of cognitive architecture in this sample, it was decided to match them with sighted. Thus the problem can be stated as the study of **"Cognitive Architecture in the Visually Impaired."**

WHO defines impairment as a permanent or transitory, psychological or anatomical loss and/or abnormality. According to Ministry of Welfare, Government of India, bulletin (1986), Visually Impaired/Handicapped are those who suffer from either of the following conditions

(a) Total absence of sight

(b) Visual acuity not exceeding 6/60 or 20/200 (snellen) in the better eye with correcting lenses

(c) Limitations of the field of vision substending an angle of 200 or worse.

It was of interest to assess how knowledge engineered in the procedural format, i.e., production rule format is utilized or influenced subsequent problem solving situations by the Visually Impaired children.

Objectives

Acquisition of knowledge formalized in rules and use of these rules in similar but different problems assess plasticity or cognitive penetrability. The objective was to examine what happens to it in the absence of an important modality of knowledge representation.

The strength of production systems, as discussed, in skill training intervention which provides training with quality was the whole idea behind the intelligent tutoring system. This, changed conceptualization of the education system in the basic academic disciplines — reading, Mathematics, Writing and Science has several capabilities as literature would show (Robert Glaser, 1988). This fostered a path to diagnose and remedy learning disabilities. Thus one important objective of this study was to find out whether a Visually Impaired child, will differ from a Sighted child after acquiring training in the solving of various tasks involving various skills.

For the education of the Visually Impaired two primary communication modes are available, namely, reading and listening. It has been shown that braille is an educational handicap in some situations (Nolan, Brothers and Morris, 1973). Others have found that orally presented material was much more effective than silent reading by blind (Bischoff 1967, Bixler 1963, Cobb 1977, Daightery 1974, Gore 1969, Halten 1976). N.K. Rai (1987) has found no significant difference between tactile medium and auditory medium for certain classes. Karrakar (1952) has emphasized the role of type of material in deciding the effectiveness of mode of presentation.

One of the important objectives of the study is thus to compare two modes of presentation of training material to the Visually Impaired children i.e. braille or audio and to outline the discrete features related to mode of presentation, Visually Impaired children were matched to a Sighted group who were also trained through two modes i.e. print or audio.

The current emphasis on integrated education, on integrating a Visually Impaired child in the community, rehabitilating him, can only lead to discriminating him or disintegrating him from the community if he doesn't understand the world like a sighted child does. The global image a person gets of the world with all the senses intact is different from discrete impressions a Visually Impaired child gets. Every Visually Impaired child may also be different from other Visually Impaired child in terms of degree of sensory loss, age of sensory loss etc. It is important, therefore, firstly to assess the cognitive architecture in the Visually Impaired children and then to overcome any lag produced by absence of vision. Training may go a long way to attain this goal. (Anderson, 1990). It involves developing a cognitive model of the skill that should be learned (eg. solving mathematics problems). It takes the form of a set of production rules that can solve a class of problems, and can later apply to other similar situations. Productions rules, being logical, simple, clear, homogeneous can be acquired through training by the Visually Impaired and can help them to become at par with the sighted in many spheres of life.

3

Methodology

The present study is aimed at studying the features of cognitive architecture in Visually Impaired children. The architecture studied is the production rule architecture, broken down in terms of content.

Considering that certain variables remain endemic to a population, the present study is planned in the framework defined by three main parameters. These are Vision Status, Intelligence and Media of Presentation.

The strategy generated for the methodology is thus, as follows:

1. Visually Impaired children in the age group 13—16 years will be administered a test of intelligence to delineate two groups comprised of high and low intelligence.
2. Sighted children in the same age group, matched on other features of the population with the Visually Impaired children will also be administered a test of intelligence to delineate similar two groups as in 1).
3. Groups of children in 1) and 2) will be provided training in the use of production rules in simple but varied situations using the braille and print script.

4. Another two groups of the same age range (13-16 yrs), one of 'high intelligence Visually Impaired children and one of high intelligence Sighted children matched on other features of the population with the four groups as in 1) and 2), will be delineated after administering the intelligence test.

5. Groups of children in 4) will be provided training in the use of production rules in simple but varied situations using the audio medium.

   The third and the fifth steps will be designated as **Phase I.**

These children will be asked to verbalize the production systems for a similar but different set of problem while solving them. This will be designated as **Phase II.** A verbatim record of each protocol will be obtained.

These protocols will be analyzed on a number of parameters, to be designated as response measures.

Objectives

The results are expected to answer the following questions:

1. Will the Visually Impaired children differ from the Sighted group on total number of words employed in a protocol description generated for a particular given task?

2. Will the higk intelligence Visually Impaired children differ from low intelligence Visually Impaired chfldren on the total number of words employed in a protocol description generated for a particular task?

3. Will the high intelligence Sighted group differ from low intelligence Sighted group on the total number of words employed in a protocol description generated for a particular task?

4. Will the Visually Impaired children differ from the Sighted group on number of production rules evolved in organizing the problem solving for a particular task?

5. Will the Visually Impaired children differ from the Sighted children on quality of production rules used to generate production system model for a particular task?
6. Will the Visually Impaired children differ from Sighted children in time taken to become proficient at use of knowledge represented in productions?
7. Will the high intelligence Visually Impaired children differ from low intelligence Visually Impaired children in time taken to become proficient at use of knowledge represented in productions?
8. Will the high intelligence Sighted group differ from the low intelligence sighted group in time taken to become proficient at use of production rules?
9. Will the Visually Impaired children differ from Sighted children in number of features used in stating the protocols for a particular task? Features are units of knowledge forming the productions. They are properties of objects represented in the problems.
10. Will the high intelligence Visually Impaired children and high intelligence Sighted children differ from low intelligence Visually Impaired group and low intelligence Sighted group in the use of features for verbalizing the protocols?
11. Will the Visually Impaired children differ from Sighted children in the use of critical features essential to reach the goal of problem solving? Critical features are those units of knowledge that organize the problem solving.
12. Will the high intelligence and low intelligence Visually Impaired children differ in the use of critical features in reaching the goal in each task?
13. Will the high intelligence and low intelligence Sighted group differ in the use of critical features in reaching the goal in each task?
14. Will the Visually Impaired children differ from sighted children in the time taken to reach the goal using the production system model?

15. Will there be a difference between the Visually Impaired children trained through braille script and Visually Impaired children trained through auditory mode in the protocols generated for a particular task?
16. Will there be a difference between the Sighted children trained through the braille script and Sighted children trained through the auditory mode in the protocols generated for a particular task?

Design

The design can now be presented as follows:-

The present research will be carried out in two Phases. The training phase, designated as Phase I. The testing phase, designated as Phase II.

Phase I Two groups of Visually Impaired children of high and low intelligence would be provided training using the braille script to make them proficient in the use of production system models.

Two groups of Sighted controls of high and low intelligence would be provided training using the print script to make them proficient in the use of production system models.

Two groups of high intelligence, one of Visually Impaired of and the other of Sighted controls would be provided training using the auditory mode of presentation to make them proficient in the use of production system models.

The tasks for training were selected on the basis of a pilot study conducted on the Visually Impaired and Sighted children. The tasks are:—

1. Mathematics	:	(Taken from Klahr et.al. 1987)
2. Pattern Matching	:	(Taken from Anderson, 1983)
3. Balance-Scale Task	:	(Task given by Piaget, taken from Klahr et.al. 1987) (Taken from Klahr et.al. 1987)
4. Reasoning	:	(Taken from Klahr et. al. 1987)
5. Circle Formation	:	(Taken from Vithopa Paknikar's Performance tests for the Blind)
6. Animal Recognition	:	(Taken from Patrick, Henry and Winston, 1977)

Total time taken to learn the production systems for each task will be noted down.

Phase II All the groups trained in the first phase will verbalize the step by step solution of twelve tasks chosen for testing the use of production system format as a result of training acquired in Phase I.

The twelve tasks that will be used to assess the success of training in terms of acquisition and application of production rules structures are

1. Mathematics I
2. Mathematics II
3. Pattern Matching I
4. Pattern Matching II
5. Parking Puzzle I
6. Size—Discrimination Puzzle II
7. Reasoning I
8. Reasoning II
9. Circle Formation I
10. Triangle Formation II
11. Animal Recognition I
12. Animal Recognition II

These twelve problems will be similar but different from the problems on which all the subjects will be trained.

The Design is illustrated on the following page:-

TABLE 3.1

THE STUDY DESIGN

	VISUALLY IMPAIRED CHILDREN			SIGHTED CHILDREN		
	TRAINED THROUGH BRAILE SCRIPT ON SIX TASKS		TRAINED THROUGH AUDITORY MODE IN ON SIX TASKS	TRAINED THROUGH PRINT SCRIPT ON SIX TASKS		TRAINED THROUGH AUDITORY MODE ON SIX TASKS
PHASE II	HIGH INTELLIGENCE GROUP	LOW NTELLIGENCE GROUP	HIGH INTELLIGENCE GROUP	HIGH INTELLIGENCE GROUP	LOW INTELLIGENCE GROUP	HIGH INTELLIGENCE GROUP
	TESTED ON TWELVE TASKS		TESTED ON TWELVE TASKS	TESTED ONTWELVE TASKS		TESTED ON TWELVE TASKS
PHASE II	HIGH INTELLIGENCE GROUP	LOW INTELLIGENCE GROUP	HIGH INTELLIGENCE GROUP	HIGH INTELLIGENCE GROUP	LOW INTELLIGENCE GROUP	HIGH INTELLIGENCE GROUP

Based as above there would be three Independent Variables

1. **Vision Status:** This will have two levels. The Visually Impaired and Sighted children. The appropriate criterion for defining Visually Impaired children will be children who are completely blind or have no pattern vision.

2. **Intelligence:** This will have 2 levels, High and Low Intelligence.

3. **Media of Presentation:** Visually Impaired children will be trained through 2 medias, braille script or auditory mode. Sighted children will also be trained through 2 medias, the print script or auditory mode.

The protocols generated by all the groups will be analyzed on a number of parameters designated as **response measures.** These are

1. **Total Number of Words:** Defined in terms of total number of words used for generating protocols for each of the twelve tasks in phase II.

2. **Number of Rules:** Defined in terms of Number of production rules used to arrive step by step at the goal of problem solving.

3. **Quality of Production Rules:** Defined in terms of statement of production rules in their condition-action format and assessed on a 5—point scale.

4. **Number of features:** Units of knowledge organized in production rules structure, representing the problem space.

5. **Critical features:** Units of knowledge organized in production rules structure, representing the problem space and essential for reaching the goal of solving each of the problem.

6. **Time:** Defined in two ways. Firstly total time taken by the Visually Impaired and Sighted children to be trained to become proficient in the use of production rules

secondly, total time taken by the Visually Impaired and Sighted children to solve the various tasks in the testing phase.

Sample

The Visually Impaired population was chosen from four residential schools for the Visually Impaired run by the Government. (N = 70+38) This covers the entire population of Visually Impaired boys in the age range of 13-16 yrs. studying in a residential set up in Delhi.

The age range selected was 13-16 years, as by this time most of the Visually Impaired children became proficient in reading and writing braille.

The Visually Impaired population was then administered an intelligence test to delineate two groups of subjects by plotting the distribution of intelligence scores. Following two groups were selected:—

1. High intelligence group comprising the top 27% of the distribution.
2. Low intelligence group comprising the lowest 27% of the distribution.

From the distribution of intelligence scores of the fourth residential school, one group, high on intelligence, was selected comprising the highest 27% of the distribution.

Similarly, the Sighted population was selected from two government schools matching the blind schools in terms of syllabus, educational system, medium of instruction, admitting children from the same socio—economic background as the Visually Impaired. (N = 104±38). A t—value between the intelligence scores of Visually Impaired children and Sighted children was not found to be significant.

The criterion used to delineate the Sighted population into three groups, one of high intelligence to be trained by print script and one by the audio script and one group of low intelligence to be trained by print script was same as used for the Visually Impaired. The final sample can be outlined as follows:

Hypotheses

Based on the research questions the following hypotheses were generated

Vision Status

1. Visually Impaired and Sighted will not differ in Total Number of words used in generating production systems for all the problem tasks in the testing phase.
2. Visually Impaired group and Sighted group will not differ in Number of Rules used in writing production systems for all the twelve tasks in the testing phase.
3. Visually Impaired children will not differ from Sighted children in the quality of production rules used to generate the production systems for all the twelve tasks in the testing phase.
4. Visually Impaired children will not differ from Sighted children in number of features used in generating protocols for all the tasks in the testing phase.
5. visually Impaired Group will not differ from Sighted group in number of critical features used in generating protocols for each problem task in the testing phase.
6. Visually Impaired children will not differ from Sighted children in the time taken to acquire knowledge represented in production systems during the training phase.
7. Visually Impaired children will not differ from Sighted children in the time taken to solve the problems using the production system models.

Intelligence

1. There will be no difference between High and Low intelligence groups in number of words used in generating protocol for all the tasks in the testing phase.
2. Visually Impaired children of high intelligence will not differ from low intelligence children in the same group in number of features making up the production rules structure generated in the testing phase.

TABLE 3.2

THE STUDY SAMPLE

VISUALLY IMPAIRED CHILDREN		SIGHTED CHILDREN			
TRAINED THROUGH BRAILE SCRIPT		TRAINED THROUGH AUDITORY MODE	TRAINED THROUGH PRINT SCRIPT		TRAINED THROUGH AUDITORY MODE
HIGH INTELLIGENCE GROUP N = 19 (HIGHEST 27%)	LOW INTELLIGENCE GROUP N = 19 (LOWEST 27%)	HIGH INTELLIGENCE GROUP N=10 (HIGHEST 27%)	HIGH INTELLIGENCE GROUP N = 26 (HIGHEST 27%)	LOW INTELLIGENCE GROUP N = 26 (LOWEST 27%)	HIGH INTELLIGENCE GROUP N = 10 (HIGHEST 27 %)
SELECTED FROM THREE RESIDENTIAL SCHOOLS FOR THE VISUALLY IMPAIRED		SELECTED FROM A FOURTH RESIDENTIAL SCHOOL FOR THE VISUALLY IMPAIRED	SELECTED FROM A GOVERNMENT SCHOOL		SELECTED FROM A GOVERNMENT SCHOOL

3. Sighted children of high intelligence will not differ from children of low intelligence in the same group in number of features making up the production rule structure generated in the testing phase.
4. Visually Impaired children of high intelligence will not differ from low intelligence children in the same group on number of critical features representing the protocols generated in the testing phase.
5. Sighted children of high intelligence will not differ from Sighted children of low intelligence in number of critical features representing the protocols generated in the testing phase.
6. High intelligence group will not differ from low intelligence group in time taken to acquire knowledge through production rules in the training phase.

Media of Presentation

1. High intelligence Visually Impaired children trained by braille script will not differ from high intelligence Visually Impaired children trained by audio medium in total number of words used in generating protocols during the testing phase.
2. Sighted children of high intelligence, trained through Print Script will not differ from Sighted children of high intelligence on total number of words used in generating protocols during the testing phase.
3. Visually Impaired children of high intelligence trained through braille script will not differ from high intelligence Visually Impaired children trained through audio medium on number of rules used in generating production systems for all the tasks in the testing phase.
4. Sighted children of high intelligence trained through print script will not differ from Sighted children trained through audio medium in number of rules used in generating production systems for all the tasks in the testing phase.

5. Visually Impaired children of high intelligence trained through braille script will not differ from Visually Impaired children of high intelligence trained through audio medium on number of features and critical features in generating production systems f of the tasks in the testing phase.
6. Sighted children of high intelligence trained through the print script will not differ from Sighted children of high intelligence trained through audio medium on number of features and critical features in generating production systems for the tasks in the testing phase.

Materials and Tasks

Intelligence

Verbal portion of Intelligence Scale for Indian Children (ISIC, Dr. Malin, 1966) adapted for the Visually Impaired by the National Institute for the Visually Handicapped, Dehradun was used for selection purpose.

Tasks for Training

Knowledge regarding step by step solution of six tasks, represented in production rule framework was imparted to all the subjects. An attempt was made to cover every aspect of the related task. To formulate and formalize these production systems, a pilot study, details of which would be presented later, was conducted. The number of rules representing a production system for a particular task differed depending on the complexity of the problem.

The tasks were selected on the basis of their suitability for both the Visually Impaired and the Sighted children and did not call for knowledge, gained only through visual modality (eg colour etc.). Three tasks, Pattern Matching, Animal Recognition and Circle Formation were tasks, in which, visual modality played a dominant role. They were specifically selected to assess the differences between Visually Impaired and Sighted children to assess the effect of knowledge overlapped through other modalities. Care was also exercised in selecting tasks which were unfamiliar but simple for both the groups. For eg. in Pattern Matching, Nonsense Figures rather than familiar patterns or Alphabets were selected because of the familiarity of Alphabets for the Sighted population.

Description of the Training Tasks

Mathematics Knowledge about Mathematical problem of subtraction with or without borrowing was engineered in the form of production rules. The rules covered a wide range of procedures from elementary mathematics. The training programme, thus, gave procedural knowledge about solving these problems step by step. [Ref. R. Neches, P. Langley and D. Klahr, 1987]. After the pilot study, the production system of this problem consisted of eight rules namely find the difference (P_1), Shift column (P_2), Find Top (P_3), Add Ten (P_4), Decrement (P_5), Shift left to borrow (P_6), Shift left across zero (P_7), Finished (P_8).

Three Series Problem The ability to reason is central to intelligence. This ability has been assessed by various people. The three term series problem assigns relative position to three objects along some linear dimension. The question is which of the three objects is at the end of one or other directions of that dimension. For example: Al is bigger than Bob. Bob is bigger than Carl. Who is smallest? This problem is used to study rational learning processes. People have also proposed several theories regarding how people solve such problems. (Hunter 1957, Noordman 1977, Stenberg 1980). It has been included in the present study because it is simple enough to be computationally tractable.

Animal Recognition The production system for this problem is different from others, in the sense, it does not specify procedural knowledge only. It is a kind of fact deducing system which states collections of known facts in form of productions and helps the children to make new conclusions. The right side of each production is a simple statement of animal name and the left side would be number of characteristics large enough to rule out any alternative identification. In operation, the user would first gather up all facts available and then scan the production list for a production which has a matching situation part. Facts flow through series of productions from left to right, thus imparting knowledge which can be later used by Visually Impaired and sighted children to recognize animals.

Circle Formation: This problem has been selected from Vithoba Paknikar Performance Tests for the Blind', which is a performance test of K.K. Paknikar (1978). The problem is based on tactual and Kinesthetic experiences and measures intelligence, viz., comprehension, memory and reasoning. The subject is to comprehend the various wooden pieces that would form a circle in the wooden case provided.

The production rules for this problem gave information regarding the circle and the formation of a circle step by step using the wooden pieces. The idea behind this tutoring was that once they learn the procedure of solving this kind of problem they can generalize it to other similar problems.

The Circle Formation test was selected because a circle is a primary and very simple form which is inherent in many things in nature which are handled by Sighted as well as by the Visually Impaired.

Pattern Matching Production rules were formulated for the task of Pattern Matching which tutored children about various figures starting from the concepts of simple vertical and horizontal lines, parallel lines and coming up to matching patterns for nonsense figures given by Vanderplas and Garvin (1959a).

Pattern Matching is the mechanism that decides which productions will apply. A fundamental claim of the production system architecture is that Pattern Matching underlies all varieties of cognition. One can model perceptual recognition by productions in which the conditions to be matched have descriptions of the patterns and the production actions involve labeling the pattern.

Fig. 3.1 illustrates part of a hypothetical pattern network for recognizing three letters, F, A and O composed of simple vertical and horizontal bars (McClleland and Rumeihart, 1981) (taken from Anderson, 1983).

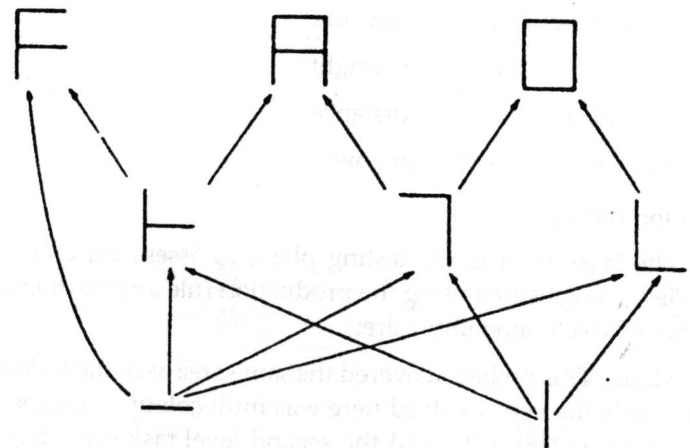

Fig. 3.1 A simple data-flow network for discussion of pattern Matching

An example of a production corresponding to 'F_1' would be of the form :

If a position contains two vertical bars, V_1 and V_2 and two horizontal bars, H_1 and H_2 and the top of V_1 is connected to the left of H_1 and the top of V_2 is connected to the right of H_2 and the middle of V_1 is connected to the left of H_2 and the middle of V_1 is connected to the left of Then the object is an F_1.

Balance Scale Task: This task was introduced by Piaget. In this task the child is presented with a two arms balance, with several pegs spaced evenly along each arm. Small disks of equal weight are placed on the pegs (only one peg on each side has weights) and the child is asked to predict the direction in which the scale will move when released. The standard method for correctly making this prediction involves the notion of torque. The number of weights on a peg is multiplied by the peg's distance from the center. If one side has the greater product, that side will go down, if the products are equal, the scale will remain balanced.

The production system of this task was modeled on Klahr and Siegler's model and gave information regarding the right behavior in the various variants of this task. An eg. of production of this task is:

If you have a balance with side
and side has the greater weight
and side has the lesser distance
then predict side will go down.

Tasks for Testing

The tasks used in the testing phase to assess the effect of knowledge engineered using the production rule approach in the absence of visual modality were:

Maths: This problem covered the same area as in the training phase. Only the task involved here was multicoloum addition in the first level (2482 + 22) and the second level task consisted of multiplication problem (831 x 31) which involved more calculations than addition.

Pattern Matching: There were two levels of this task. Two nonsense figures were selected for this problem area. The tasks involved recognizing and naming these figures. The first level consisted of a four-line figure and the second level consisted of a twelve line figure.

Puzzles: In this area two problems were selected. The first one called the parking puzzle had two types of knobs. One type of knobs, which were three in number had a pin on it and the other three had no pin on it. The subjects had to discriminate between these knobs and bring one type of knobs from right to left and the other type from left to right. There was a path in between the two types of knobs to slide them and another path in the middle to part them in order to achieve the task.

The second problem in this area was called the size discrimination puzzle. It consisted of a rectangular board having 5 slots having the same shape but different in size. The size of the slots was increasing serially i.e. the first slot on the left was smallest and the last slot on the right was the biggest. The subjects were provided with 5 wooden pieces all having the same shape (i.e. of Rabbit but of different sizes). The task involved recognizing and fitting the right wooden piece in the right slot.

Reasoning: Two levels of reasoning problem, similar to the one the subjects were trained on was presented to the subjects. The first level involved three series and the second level, being more complex involved four series problem. The task involved solving the problem in terms of reasoning logic.

Circle Formation and Triangle Formation: These problem were also similar to the training problem. The Circle Formation problem was simple and involved 4 triangle pieces, 5 rectangle pieces and 5 semi circles. The subject had to fit these pieces together to form a circle in the wooden case provided along with wooden pieces. The triangle formation problem was similar to the circle formation except for the shape to be constructed from the wooden pieces was that of a triangle.

Animal Recognition, There were two levels of this problem. This problem was based again on the one the subjects were trained on. The problem involved recognizing a specific bird for the first level and a Reptile in the second level by touching stuffed models of these animals.

Procedure

The procedure followed can be divided in three sections: the pilot study, the training and the testing section.

Pilot Study

Before the selection of six tasks for training, a pilot study, involving 20 Visually Impaired children and 20 Sighted children was carried out. The sample for this study was taken from two schools and was incidental random sample of various age ranges.

The children were given various tasks to solve and were instructed to write the solutions of these tasks step by step. On the basis of this pilot study, it was found that the most suitable age range that could be included in the study was 13-16 years,as younger Visually Impaired children could not read and write braille properly.

It was also found that children gave solution of tasks in steps which did not have any logic. Each child differed from the other in the pattern of writing solutions. Some tasks were found to be extremely difficult for the Visually Impaired and some easy. Therefore, on the basis of suitability for both the groups, six tasks were selected for the actual study. From the solutions given by the subjects and also from other sources, knowledge related to these six tasks was engineered or formalized in a Production Rule Structure which was uniform and logical for all the subjects.

Training

Training through braille and print script Two groups of Visually Impaired children (High and Low in intelligence) and two groups of sighted children (High and Low in Intelligence) were presented written material individually. The material consisted of production systems for each of the six tasks. These production systems were to be understood and learned by the four groups.

Each subject was asked to take as much time as he wished in learning the systems. The total time taken to learn the production rules for each task was noted down. The subjects were asked to inform the researcher when they finished learning. At the end the subjects were asked to write a production rule from each of six production systems to test whether they had learned the logic of rules well or not. If a subject was unable to write the production rule correctly, he was instructed to learn it for some more time. The criterion for mastery was the reproduction of production rules in a correct format. To counteract the fatigue effect, the subjects were presented only one task each day thus, each subject participated in the training phase for six days.

Instructions

The general instructions for this phase were:

> "You would be presented some material that you have to read and learn, taking care of the format of the rule and the knowledge represented in it regarding solution of various tasks. Be sure that you understand everything and then learn it well enough to write any rule, when asked, from the material you have just learned in its correct format and with all the represented knowledge. You can take as much time as you want."

Training through audio medium The third group of Visually Impaired Children and of Sighted children, both of high intelligence were trained in the use of production systems through audio medium. Otherwise the instructions and procedure used for this group were same as above.

Teuting

In this phase all the Visually Impaired children and blindfolded sighted children were tested individually. Each subject was given each of the twelve tasks, one by one to solve it and speak out the solution organized in production rules, i.e., they were asked to follow the same format of reporting as they had learned in the training phase. To counteract the fatigue effect, each subject was given only one task to solve each day. The total time taken to solve the problem was noted down.

Instruct ions

The general instructions for this phase were:

> "You have to solve some problems presented to you one by one and report verbally how you are solving these problems. Try to give the solution procedure in the same rule format as you have learned in training phase."

Following these general instructions, task related specific instructions were given at the time of testing for each task.

The protocols generated by the subjects were written down by the researcher and later analyzed in terms of parameters designated as response measures, which have been discussed earlier.

4

Results

Following response measures were generated from analysis of the production system protocols.

Response Measures

Number of Words

Total number of words used by both the Visually Impaired and Sighted children in expressing the solution of each problem task in production system model were counted separately and recorded.

Quality of Production Rules

Quality of Production rules was evaluated on a 5-point scale [1 (poor) to 5 (superior)]. Two independent judges judged the quality of production rules and the general agreement between the two judges was taken as a measure of inter-rater reliability. The criterion used for judgement was the correct statement of the production. rule in condition-action (if-then) format.

Number of Rules

Total number of rules used to generate a production System for each task were counted both for the Visually Impaired and Sighted subjects.

Time Taken in Training and Solving Problems

Total time taken, in seconds, to learn the production systems for each of six problem tasks during the training phase and total time taken to solve twelve problem task using production rules in the testing phase was recorded.

Number of Features

Total number of features related to the concept of the problem represented in the production system for each problem task during the testing phase were counted for both the samples.

Critical Features

Total number of critical features, i.e. features essential for reaching the solution of each problem task, as represented in the production systems were delineated and noted down for both the samples.

Vision Status

The main effect of vision status on number of words employed was found to be significant for Pattern Matching I, Parking puzzle I, Animal Recognition I and Animal Recognition II. Main effect of intelligence was found to be significant for eleven tasks. Only with respect to Pattern Matching I it was not significant. The interaction effect between vision status x intelligence was found to be significant for the task pattern matching I, Pattern Matching II, Parking Puzzle, Size—Discrimination Puzzle, Reasoning I and Reasoning II and Circle Formation. Table number 4.1-4.12 below present the summary of the effects for each problem task. Figs. 4.1-4.12 present the interaction effects for the tasks as mentioned above.

TABLE : 4.1

SUMMARY ANOVA WITH INTELLIGENCE (2 LEVELS) AND VISION STATUS (2 LEVELS) ON NUMBER OF WORDS EMPLOYED IN MATHS I

SOURCES OF VARIATION	SUM OF SQUARES	dF	M Square	F
VISION STATUS (VISUALLY IMPAIRED AND SIGHTED)	9805.566	1	9805.566	1.734
INTELLIGENCE (HIGH AND LOW)	421296.266	1	421296.266	74.494**
TWO WAY INTERACTION (VISION STATUS (INTELLIGENCE)	48.042	1	48.042	.008
RESIDUAL	508988.094	90	5655.423	
TOTAL	**940137.968**	**93**	**10109.010**	

** Sig. at .01 level.

TABLE : 4.2

SUMMARY ANOVA WITH INTELLIGENCE (2 LEVELS) AND VISION STATUS(2 LEVELS) ON NUMBER OF WORDS EMPLOYED IN MATHS II

SOURCES OF VARIATION	SUM OF SQUARES	dF	N Square	F
VISION STATUS (VISUALLY IMPAIREDAND SIGHTED)	11.399	1	11.399	.003
INTELLIGENCE (HIGH AND LOW)	163639.191	1	163639.191	40.748**
TWO WAY INTERACTION (VISION STATUS (INTELLIGENCE)	10758.439	1	10758.439	2.679
RESIDUAL	301432.077	90	4015.912	
TOTAL	**535841.106**	**93**	**5761.732**	

** Sig. at .01 level.

TABLE : 4.3

SUMMARY ANOVA WITH INTELLIGENCE (2 LEVELS) AND VISION STATUS (2 LEVELS) ON NUMBER OF WORDS EMPLOYED IN PATTERN MATCHING I

SOURCES OF VARIATION	SUM OF SQUARES	dF	M Square	F
VISION STATUS (VISUALLY IMPAIREDAND SIGHTED)	15275.842	1	15275.842	10.545**
INTELLIGENCE (HIGH AND LOW)	3288.681	1	3288.681	2.270
TWO WAY INTERACTION (VISION STATUS INTELIGENCE)	7857.769	1	7857.769	5.424*
RESIDUAL	130376.814	90		
TOTAL	**156799.106**	**93**		

* Sig. at .05 level.

** Sig. at .01 level.

TABLE : 4.4

SUMMARY ANOVA WITH INTELLIGENCE (2 LEVELS) AND VISION STATUS (2 LEVELS) ON NUMBER OF WORDS EMPLOYED IN PATTERN MATCHING II

SOURCES OF VARIATION	SUM OF SQUARES	dF	M Square	F
VISION STATUS (VISUALLY IMPAIREDAND SIGHTED)	1253.694	1	1253.694	.382
INTELLIGENCE (HIGH AND LOW)	283470.681	1	283470.681	86.421**
TWO WAY INTERACTION (VISION STATUS X INTELLIGENCE)	29357.620	1	29357.620	8.950**
RESIDUAL	295209.282	90	3280.103	
TOTAL	**609291.277**	**93**	**6551.519**	

** Sig. at .01 level.

TABLE : 4.5

SUMMARY ANOVA WITH INTELLIGENCE (2 LEVELS) AND VISION STATUS (2 LEVELS) ON NUMBER OF WORDS EMPLOYED IN PUZZLE I

SOURCES OF VARIATION	SUM OF SQUARES	dF	N Square	F
VISION STATUS (VISUALLY IMPAIRED AND SIGHTED)	7860.941	1	7860.941	4□395*
INTELLIGENCE (HIGH AND LOW)	29279.585	1	29279.585	16.372**
TWO WAY INTERACTION (VISION STATUS X INTELLIGENCE)	38480.117	1	38480.117	21.516**
RESIDUAL	160957.325	90		
TOTAL	**236577.968**	**93**		

* Sig. at .05 level.

** Sig. at .01 level.

TABLE : 4.6

SUMMARY ANOVA WITH INTELLIGENCE (2 LEVELS) AND VISION STATUS (2 LEVELS) ON NUMBER OF WORDS EMPLOYED IN PUZZLE II

SOURCES OF VARIATION	SUM OF SQUARES	dF	U Square	F
VISION STATUS (VISUALLY IMPAIRED AND SIGHTED)	2780.109	1	2780.109	1.734
INTELLIGENCE (HIGH AND LOW)	87199.670	1	87199.670	54.378**
TWO WAY INTERACTION (VISION STATUS X INTELLIGENCE)	22180.912	1	22180.912	13.832**
RESIDUAL	144321.235	90	1603.569	
TOTAL	**256481.926**	**93**	**2757.870**	

** Sig. at .01 level.

TABLE : 4.7

SUMMARY ANOVA WITH INTELLIGENCE (2 LEVELS) AND VISION STATUS (2 LEVELS) ON NUMBER OF WORDS EMPLOYED IN REASONING I

SOURCES OF VARIATION	SUM OF SQUARES	dF	M Square	F
VISION STATUS (VISUALLY IMPAIRED AND SIGHTED)	30.946	1	30.946	.051
INTELLIGENCE (HIGH AND LOW)	9520.383	1	9520.383	15.707**
TWO WAY INTERACTION (VISION STATUS X INTELLIGENCE)	5903.478	1	5903.478	9.739**
RESIDUAL	54552.470	90	606.139	
TOTAL	70007.277	93	752.766	

** Sig. at .01 level.

TABLE : 4.8

SUMMARY ANOVA WITH INTELLIGENCE (2 LEVELS) AND VISION STATUS (2 LEVELS) ON NUMBER OF WORDS EMPLOYED IN REASONING II

SOURCES OF VARIATION	SUM OF SQUARES	dF	M Square	F
VISION STATUS (VISUALLY IMPAIRED AND SIGHTED)	106.890	1	106.890	.329
INTELLIGENCE (HIGH AND LOW)	8906.649	1	8906.649	27.413**
TWO WAY INTERACTION (VISION STATUS X INTELLIGENCE)	3692.084	1	3692.084	11.363**
RESIDUAL	29241.835	90	324.909	
TOTAL	41947.457	93	451.048	

** Sig. at .01 level.

TABLE : 4.9

SUMMARY ANOVA WITH INTELLIGENCE (2 LEVELS) AND VISION STATUS (2 LEVELS) ON NUMBER OF WORDS EMPLOYED IN CIRCLE FORMATION

SOURCES OF VARIATION	SUM OF SQUARES	dF	N Square	F
VISION STATUS (VISUALLY IMPAIRED AND SIGHTED)	960.899	1	960.899	.817
INTELLIGENCE (HIGH AND LOW)	30420.011	1	30420.011	25.879**
TWO WAY INTERACTION (VISION STATUS X INTELLIGENCE)	16947.459	1	16947.459	14.4.17**
RESIDUAL	105793.940	90	1175.488	
TOTAL	**154122.309**	**93**	**1657.229**	

** Sig. at .01 level.

TABLE : 4.10

SUMMARY ANOVA WITH INTELLIGENCE (2 LEVELS) AND VISION STATUS(2 LEVELS) ON NUMBER OF WORDS EMPLOYED IN TRIANGLE FORMATION

SOURCES OF VARIATION	SUM OF SQUARES	dF	N Square	F
VISION STATUS (VISUALLY IMPAIRED AND SIGHTED)	845.905	1	845.905	.150
INTELLIGENCE (HIGH AND LOW)	31362.649	1	31362.649	5.573*
TWO WAY INTERACTION (VISION STATUS X INTELLIGENCE)	4778.231	1	4778.231	.849
RESIDUAL	506490.545	90	5627.673	
TOTAL	**543477.330**	**93**	**5843.842**	

* Sig. at .05 level.

TABLE : 4.11

SUMMARY ANOVA WITH INTELLIGENCE (2 LEVELS) AND VISION STATUS (2 LEVELS) ON NUMBER OF WORDS EMPLOYED IN ANIMAL RECOGNITION I

SOURCES OF VARIATION	SUM OF SQUARES	dF	M Square	F
VISION STATUS (VISUALLY IMPAIRED AND SIGHTED)	1602.152	1	1602.152	6.260**
INTELLIGENCE (HIGH AND LOW)	5138.564	1	5138.564	20.078**
TWO WAY INTERACTION (VISION STATUS X INTELLIGENCE)	89.619	1	89.619	.350
RESIDUAL	23033.378	90	255.926	
TOTAL	**29863.713**	**93**	**321.115**	

** Sig. at .01 levels.

TABLE : 4.12

SUMMARY ANOVA WITH INTELLIGENCE (2 LEVELS) AND VISION STATUS(2 LEVELS) ON NUMBER OF WORDS EMPLOYED IN ANIMAL RECOGNITION II

SOURCES OF VARIATION	SUM OF SQUARES	dF	M Square	F
VISION STATUS (VISUALLY IMPAIRED AND SIGHTED)	1049.922	1	1049.922	7.592**
INTELLIGENCE (HIGH AND LOW)	5469.032	1	5469.032	39.547**
TWO WAY INTERACTION (VISION STATUS X INTELLIGENCE	5.201	1	5.201	.038
RESIDUAL	12446.323	90	138.292	
TOTAL	**18970.479**	**93**	**203.984**	

** Sig. at .01 level.

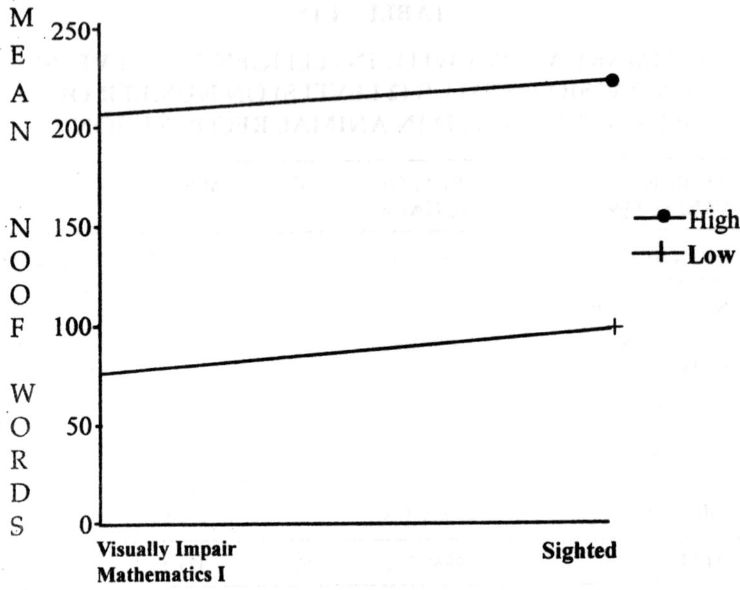

Fig. 4.1 Interaction bet. Vision Status and Intelligence on no. of words.

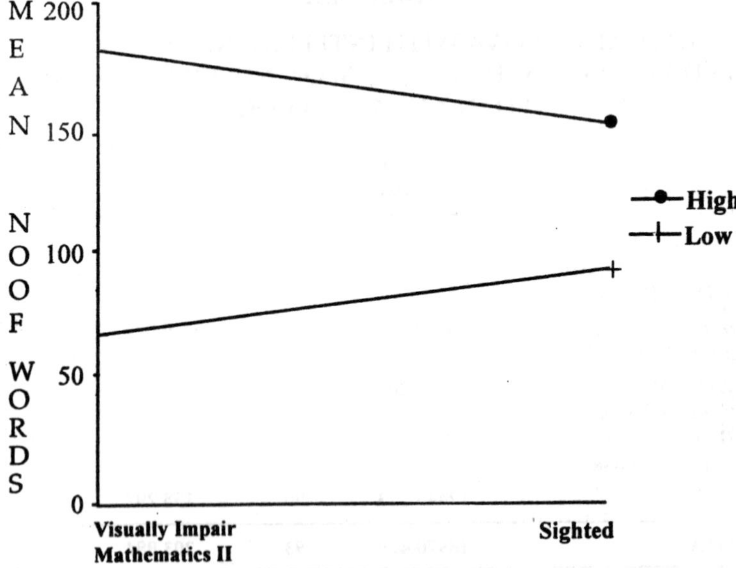

Fig. 4.2 Interaction bet. Vision Status and Intelligence on no. of words.

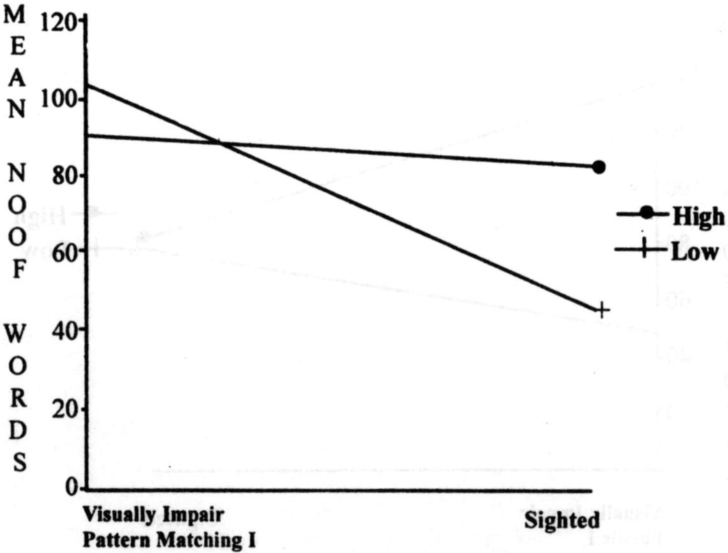

Fig. 4.3 Interaction bet. Vision Status and Intelligence on no. of words.

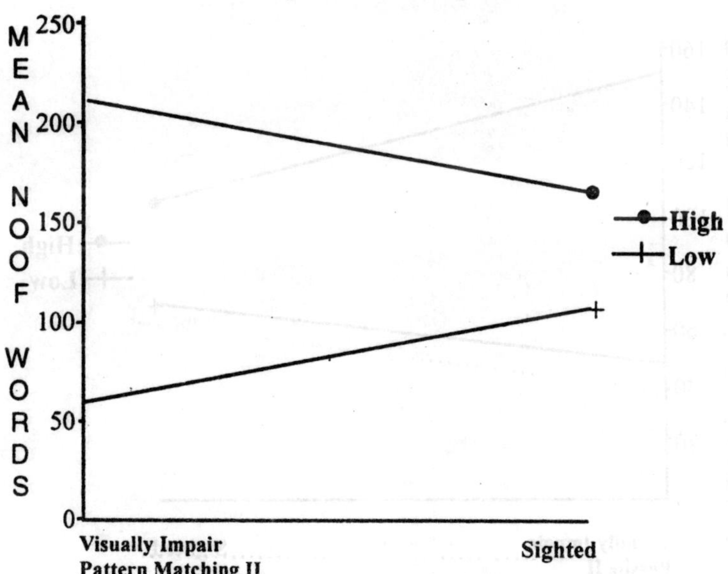

Fig. 4.4 Interaction bet. Vision Status and Intelligence on no. of words.

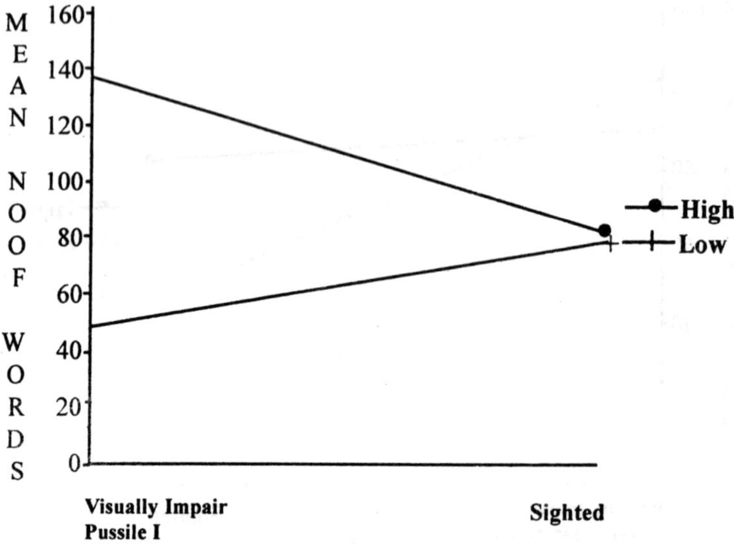

Fig. 4.5 Interaction bet. Vision Status and Intelligence on no. of words.

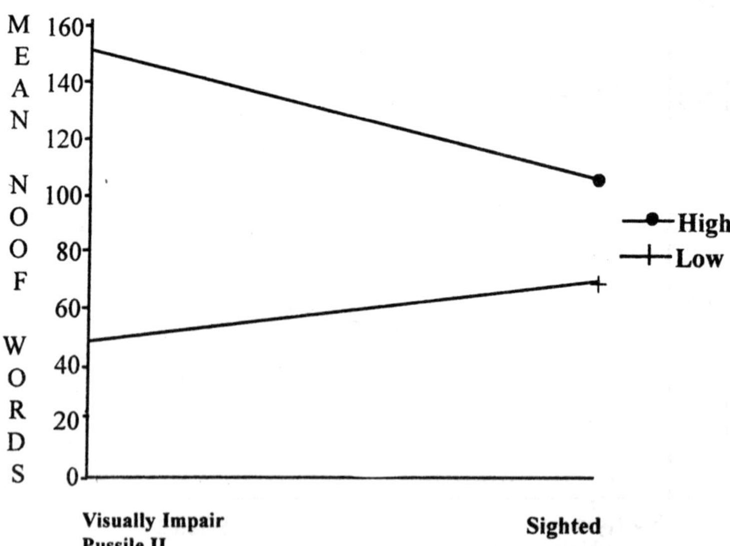

Fig. 4.6 Interaction bet. Vision Status and Intelligence on no. of words.

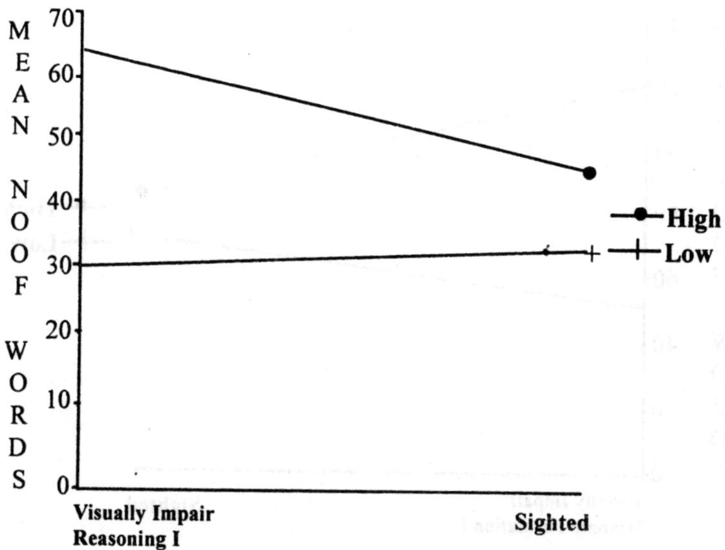

Fig. 4.7 Interaction bet. Vision Status and Intelligence on no. of words.

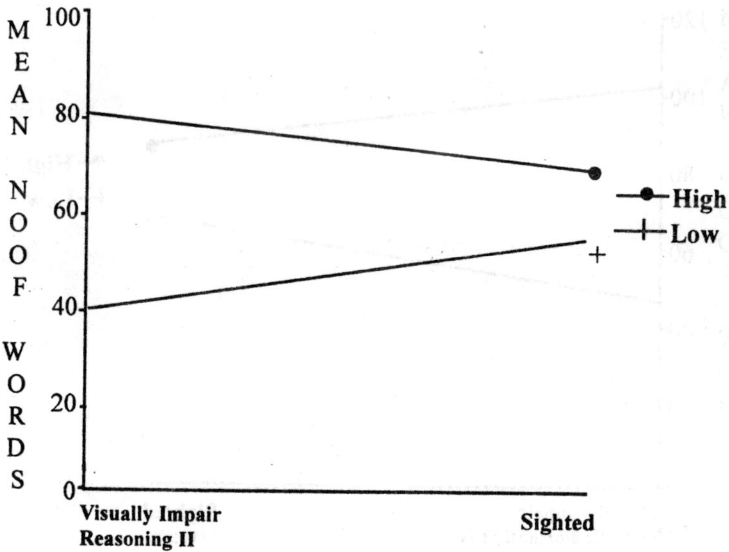

Fig. 4.8 Interaction bet. Vision Status and Intelligence on no. of words.

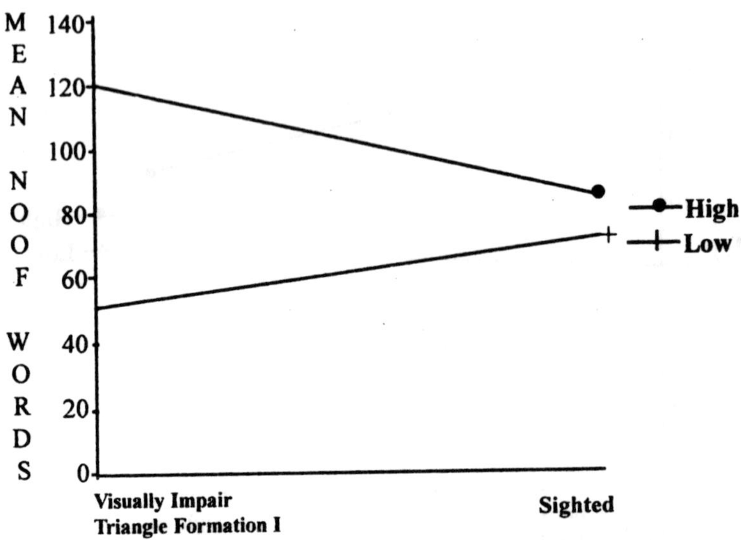

Fig. 4.9 Interaction bet. Vision Status and Intelligence on no. of words.

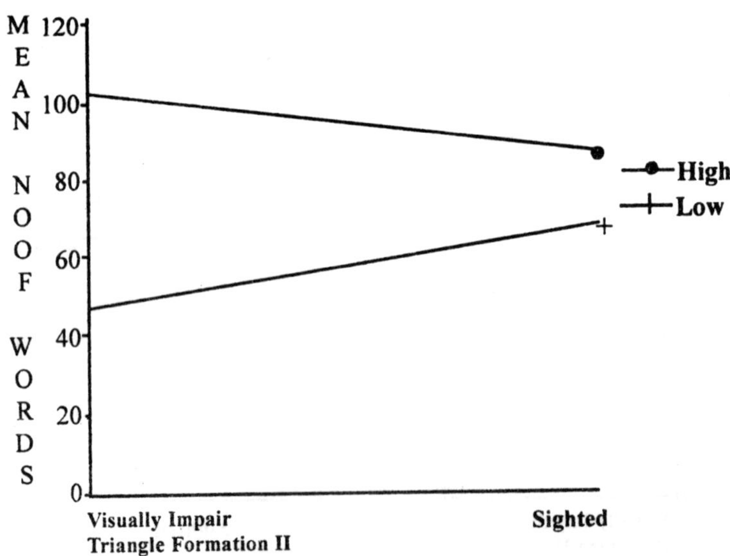

Fig. 4.10 Interaction bet. Vision Status and Intelligence on no. of words.

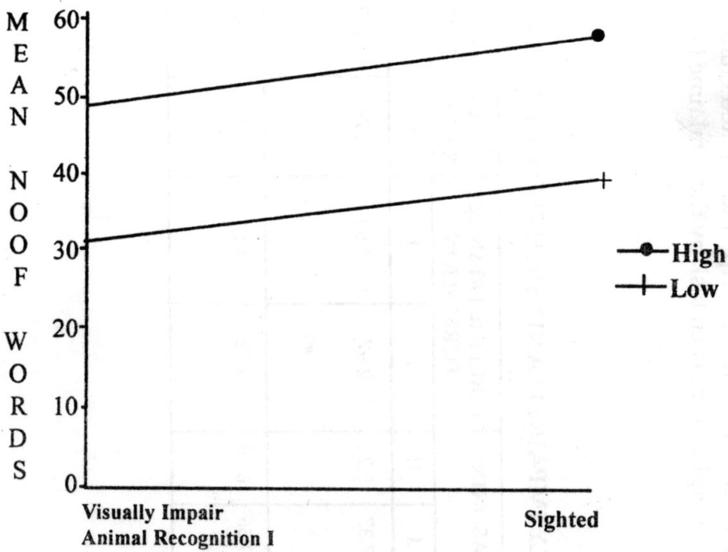

Fig. 4.11 Interaction bet. Vision Status and Intelligence on no. of words.

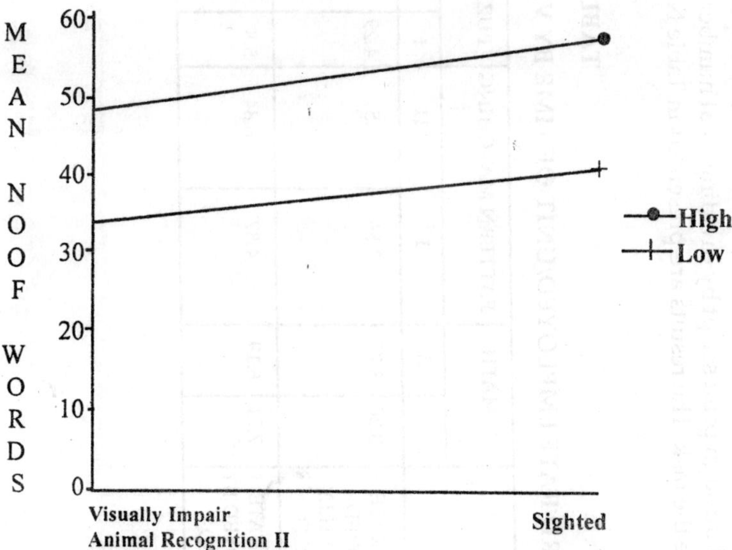

Fig. 4.12 Interaction bet. Vision Status and Intelligence on no. of words.

Word rate per unit was found for Visually Impaired trained through braille script and Sighted children trained through print script by dividing total number of words employed in each task by the total time taken to solve the task. The results are presented in Table No. 4.13.

TABLE : 4.13

WORD RATE EMPLOYED/UNIT OF TIME BY VISUALLY IMPAIRED AND SIGHTED CHILDREN

TASKS	MATH		PATTERN MATCHING		PUZZLE		REASONING		CIRCLE & TRIANGLE FORMATION		ANIMAL RECOGNITION	
	I	II	I	II	I	II	I	II	I	II	I	II
WORD RATE EMPLOYED BY VISUALLY IMPAIRED	3.80	3.72	3.86	4.51	4.29	4.00	7.37	5.24	2.97	2.90	2.76	3.37
WORD RATE EMPLOYED BY SIGHTED	7.71	6.19	4.87	6.84	5.8	5.13	9.56	6.90	4.12	4.81	3.22	5.85

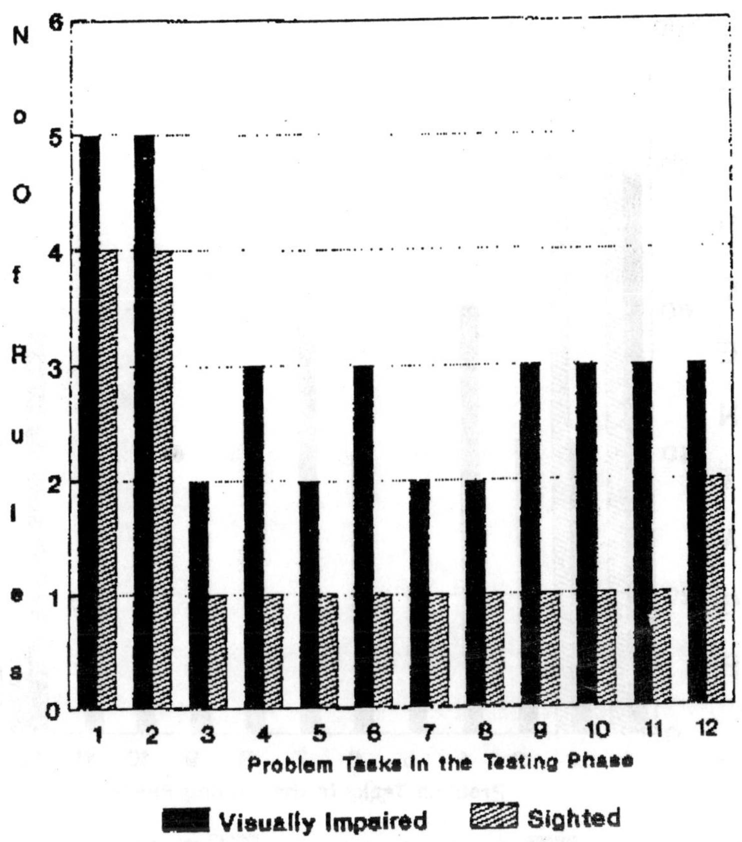

Fig. 4.13 Number of Rules used by Visually Impaired and Sighted.

Fig.4.13 shows that Visually **Impaired** subjects made use of a larger number of rules than the Sighted subjects. Fig.4.14 presents percentage of Visually Impaired and Sighted subjects employing more than one rule for generating production systems for the twelve problem tasks during the testing phase.

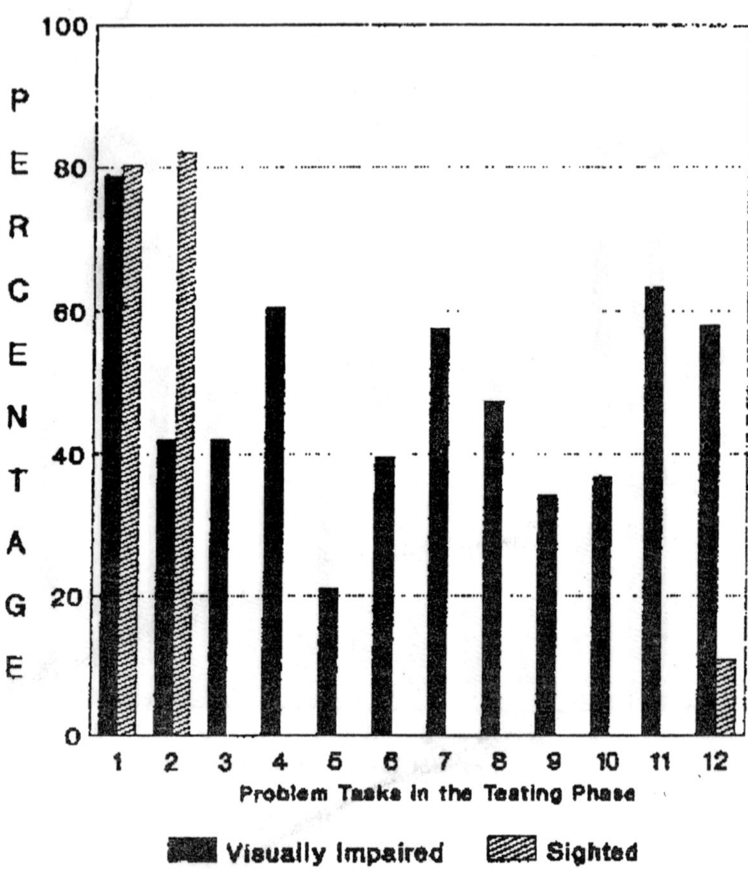

Fig. 4.14 Percentage of Visually Impaired and Sighted using more than one rule

The above figure shows that the percentage of sighted subjects using more than one rule was less than that of Visually Impaired subjects for all the tasks.

Quality of Production Rules did not differ for the two samples in eleven out of twelve tasks (Table 4.14). Only with respect to Triangle Formation the difference between two samples was observed.

TABLE : 4.14

T-VALUES FOR DIFFERENCE BETWEEN THE MEANS ON QUALITY OF PRODUCTIONS OF VISUALLY IMPAIRED AND SIGHTED SUBJECTS

TASKS	MATH		PATTERN MATCHING		PUZZLE		REASONING		CIRCLE & TRIANGLE FORMATION		ANIMAL RECOGNITION	
	I	II	I	II	I	II	I	II	I	II	I	II
t-VALUES	-.54	-1.49	-.95	-.71	-1.28	-1.83	-.30	.43	-1.16	-2.87**	-1.24	-.01

** Sig. at .01 level.

Visually impaired and sighted children did not differ significantly on the number of features use in writing the production systems in eleven out of twelve tasks. The difference between two samples was significant only for the task Animal Recognition I (Table 4.15).

TABLE 4.15

T-VALUE8 FOR DIFFERENCE BETWEEN MEANS ON NUMBER OF FEATURES EMPLOYED IN EACH TASK BY VISUALLY IMPAIRED AND SIGHTED CHILDREN

S.NO.	PROBLEM TASK	GROUP	MEAN	SD	df	t-VALUE
1	2	3	4	5	6	7
1.	MATHS I	VISUALLY IMPAIRED	9.58	5.515	92	-1.39
		SIGHTED	11.11	5.00		
2.	MATHS II	VISUALLY IMPAIRED	8.55	4.18	92	-1.77
		SIGHTED	9.91	3.23		
3.	PATTERN MATCHING I	VISUALLY IMPAIRED	9.63	3.50	92	1.70
		SIGHTED	8.59	2.455		
4.	PATTERN MATCHING II	VISUALLY IMPAIRED	12.16	6.54	92	1.80
		SIGHTED	10.36	3.02		
5.	PUZZLE I	VISUALLY IMPAIRED	8.42	5.91	92	.08
		SIGHTED	8.55	8.83		
6.	PUZZLE II	VISUALLY IMPAIRED	8.10	4.28	92	-.51
		SIGHTED	8.48	2.94		
7.	REASONING I	VISUALLY IMPAIRED	6.34	2.80	92	-1.28
		SIGHTED	7.00	2.18		
8.	REASONING II	VISUALLY IMPAIRED	5.34	2.122	92	-.99
		SIGHTED	5.77	1.98		

(Contd...)

1	2	3	4	5	6	7
9.	CIRCLE FORMATION I	VISUALLY IMPAIRED	9.71	6.38	92	1.41
		SIGHTED	8.36	2.73		
10.	TRAIANGLE FORMATION II	VISUALLY IMPAIRED	8.08	4.90	92	.79
		SIGHTED	7.48	2.38		
11.	ANIMAL RECOGNITION I	VISUALLY IMPAIRED	7.14	2.63	92	2.45**
		SIGHTED	9.13	2.51		
12.	ANIMAL RECOGNITION II	VISUALLY IMPAIRED	7.79	2.28	92	-1.42
		SIGHTED	8.52	2.54		

** Sig. at .01 level.

Visually impaired and sighted children did not differ on the critical features in ten out of twelve tasks (Table 4.16). Only with respect to Maths I and Maths II the difference was significant.

Tables 4.17 to 4.22 present summary ANOVA for 2x2 factorial design with vision status at two levels, Visually Impaired and Sighted and Intelligence at two levels High and Low intelligence. Main effect of vision status and intelligence for all the six tasks during the training phase on time taken in training was found to be significant.

Interaction effect between Visually Impaired x Intelligence was significant for tasks Pattern Matching, Circle Formation only.

Table 4.23 gives t—values for difference between means of Visually Impaired and Sighted children on time taken to solve the problems. t—values for all the tasks were found to be significant.

TABLE : 4.16

T—VALUES FOR DIFFERENCE BETWEEN MEANS ON NUMBER OF CRITICAL FEATURES EMPLOYED IN EACH TASK BY VISUALLY IMPAIRED AND SIGHTED CHILDREN

S.NO.	PROBLEM TASK	GROUP	MEAN	SD	df	t-VALUE
1	2	3	4	5	6	7
1.	MATHS I	VISUALLY IMPAIRED	4.82	2.65	92	-2.55
		SIGHTED	6.25	2.70		
2.	MATHS II	VISUALLY IMPAIRED	4.10	2.21	92	-3.32
		SIGHTED	5.66	2.34		
3.	PATTERN MATCHING 1	VISUALLY IMPAIRED	5.84	2.42	92	1.13
		SIGHTED	5.32	2.04		
4.	PATTERN MATCHING II	VISUALLY IMPAIRED	6.60	2.86	92	-.12
		SIGHTED	6.68	2.74		
5.	PUZZLE I	VISUALLY IMPAIRED	3.84	2.26	92	-1.16
		SIGHTED	4.32	1.73		
6.	PUZZLE II	VISUALLY IMPAIRED	4.63	2.71	92	-.06
		SIGHTED	4.66	1.97		
7.	REASONING I	VISUALLY IMPAIRED	3.81	1.59	92	-.97
		SIGHTED	5.23	8.92		
8.	REASONING II	VISUALLY IMPAIRED	3.55	1.57	92	-.11
		SIGHTED	3.59	1.67		
9.	CIRCLE FORMATION I	VISUALLY IMPAIRED	4.37	2.25	92	-1.78
		SIGHTED	5.18	2.12		

(Contd...)

1	2	3	4	5	6	7
10.	TRAIANGLE FORMATION II	VISUALLY IMPAIRED	3.76	2.31	92	-1.21
		SIGHTED	4.27	1.72		
11.	ANIMAL RECOGNITION I	VISUALLY IMPAIRED	6.26	2.09	92	-.13
		SIGHTED	6.32	2.56		
12.	ANIMAL RECOGNITION II	VISUALLY IMPAIRED	5.895	2.02	92	-.27
		SIGHTEDs	6.018	2.27		

** Sig. at .01 Level.

TABLE : 4.17

SUMMARY ANOVA WITH INTELLIGENCE (2 LEVELS) AND VISION STATUS (2 LEVELS) ON TIME TAKEN IN TRAINING FOR MATHS

SOURCES OF VARIATION	SUM OF SQUARES	dF	M Square	F
VISION STATUS (VISUALLY IMPAIRED AND SIGHTED)	3214.530	1	3214.530	26.218**
INTELLIGENCE (HIGH AND LOW)	17559.116	1	17559.116	143.214**
TWO WAY INTERACTION (VISION STATUS X INTELLIGENCE)	123.927		123.927	1.011
RESIDUAL	11034.716	90	122.608	
TOTAL	**31932.289**	**93**	**343.358**	

** Sig. at .01 level.

TABLE : 4.18

SUMMARY ANOVA WITH INTELLIGENCE (2 LEVELS) AND VISION STATUS (2 LEVELS) ON TIME TAKEN IN TRAINING FOR PATTERN MATCHING

SOURCES OF VARIATION	SUM OF SQUARES	dF	M Square	F
VISION STATUS (VISUALLY IMPAIRED AND SIGHTED)	1138.159	1	1138.159	12.221**
INTELLIGENCE (HIGH AND LOW)	11523.428	1	11523.428	123.737**
TWO WAY INTERACTION (VISION STATUS X INTELLIGENCE)	1023.082	1	1023.082	10.986**
RESIDUAL	8381.530	90	93.128	
TOTAL	**22066.198**	**93**	**237.271**	

** Sig. at .01 level.

TABLE : 4.19

SUMMARY ANOVA WITH INTELLIGENCE (2 LEVELS) AND VISION STATUS (2 LEVELS) ON TIME TAKEN IN TRAINING FOR BALANCE SCALE TASK

SOURCES OF VARIATION	SUM OF SQUARES	dF	M Square	F
VISION STATUS (VISUALLY IMPAIREDAND SIGHTED)	2830.434	1	2830.434	38.702**
INTELLIGENCE (HIGH AND LOW)	9052.865	1	9052.865	123.784**
TWO WAY INTERACTION (VISION STATUS X INTELLIGENCE)	184.812	1	184.812	2.527
RESIDUAL	6582.096	90	73.134	
TOTAL	**18650.207**	**93**	**200.540**	

** Sig. at .01 level.

TABLE : 4.20

SUMMARY ANOVA WITH INTELLIGENCE (2 LEVELS) AND VISION STATUS (2 LEVELS) ON TIME TAKEN IN TRAINING FOR REASONING

SOURCES OF VARIATION	SUM OF SQUARES	dF	M Square	F
VISION STATUS (VISUALLY IMPAIRED AND SIGHTED)	873.100	1	873.100	12.580**
INTELLIGENCE (HIGH AND LOW)	6187.769	1	6187.769	89.153**
TWO WAY INTERACTION (VISION STATUS X INTELLIGENCE)	102.664	1	102.664	1.479
RESIDUAL	6246.525	90	69.406	
TOTAL	**13410.057**	**93**	**144.194**	

** Sig. at .01 level.

TABLE : 4.21

SUMMARY ANOVA WITH INTELLIGENCE (2 LEVELS) AND VISION STATUS (2 LEVELS) ON TIME TAKEN IN TRAINING FOR CIRCLE FORMATION

SOURCES OF VARIATION	SUM OF SQUARES	dF	M Square	F
VISION STATUS. (VISUALLY IMPAIRED AND SIGHTED)	2279.230	1	2279.230	16.343**
INTELLIGENCE (HIGH AND LOW)	12555.779	1	12555.779	90.033**
TWO WAY INTERACTION (VISION STATUS X INTELLIGENCE)	892.196	1	892.196	6.398**
RESIDUAL	12551.220	90	139.458	
TOTAL	**28278.425**	**93**	**304.069**	

** Sig. at .01 level.

TABLE : 4.22

SUMMARY ANOVA WITH INTELLIGENCE (2 LEVELS) AND VISION STATUS (2 LEVELS) ON TIME TAKEN IN TRAINING FOR ANIMAL RECOGNITION

SOURCES OF VARIATION	SUM OF SQUARES	000dF	M Square	F
VISION STATUS (VISUALLY IMPAIRED AND SIGHTED)	3149.651	1	3149.651	24.444**
INTELLIGENCE (HIGH AND LOW)	14145.593	1	14145.593	109.781**
TWO WAY INTERACTION (VISION STATUS X INTELLIGENCE)	458.359	1	458.359	3.557
RESIDUAL	11596.766	90	128.853	
TOTAL	**29350.369**	**93**	**315.595**	

** Sig. at .01 level.

TABLE : 4.23

T-VALUES FOR DIFFERENCE BETWEEN THE MEANS ON THE TAKEN TO SOLVE THE PROBLEM TASKS BY VISUALLY IMPAIRED AND SIGHTED SUBJECTS

TASKS	MATH		PATTERN MATCHING		PUZZLE		REASONING		CIRCLE & TRIANGLE FORMATION		ANIMAL RECOGNITION	
	I	II	I	II	I	II	I	II	I	II	I	II
t-VALUES	3.01**	2.98*	2.51*	2.71**	1.99*	2.36*	2.04*	2.11*	2.80**	2.92**	2.64**	2.66**

* Sig. at .05 level.

** Sig. at .01 level.

Intelligence

On reference to Table 4.1 to 4.12, Intellige1~ce as a main effect was observed to be significant for eleven out of twelve task for the variable Number of words. The tasks were; Maths I ($F = 74.494$, df = 1,90, $p < .01$); Maths II ($F = 40.748$, df = 1,90, $p < .01$); Pattern Matching II ($F = 86.421$, df = 1,90, $p < .01$); Puzzle I ($F = 16.372$, df = 1,90, $P < .01$); Puzzle II ($F = 54.378$, df = 1,90, $P < .01$); Reasoning I ($F = 15.707$, df = 1,90, $P < .01$); Reasoning II (F⇐ 27.413, df = 1,90, $P < .01$); Circle Formation ($F = 25.879$, df 1,90, $P < .01$), Triangle Formation ($F = 5.573$, df 1,90, $P < .05$); Animal Recognition I ($F = 20.078$, df = 1,90, $P < .01$); Animal Recognition II ($F = 39.547$, df = 1,90, $P < .01$).

On reference to the same tables the Interaction effect between Visually Impaired x Intelligence for total no. of words was found to be significant for the task Pattern Matching I and II ($F = 5.424$, df = 1,90, $P < .05$), ($F = 8.950$, df = 1,90, $P < .01$); Puzzle I ($F = 21.516$, df = 1,90, $P < .01$); Puzzle II ($F = 13.832$, df = 1,90, $P < .01$); Reasoning I ($F = 9.739$, df = 1,90, $P < .01$); Reasoning II ($F = 11.363$, df = 1,90, $P < .01$) and Circle Formation ($F = 14.417$, df = 1,90, $p < .01$).

To test the difference between the means of High and Low intelligence Visually Impaired groups and the means of High and Low intelligence sighted groups for number of features employed in generating production systems for all the twelve tasks, a t—test (independent samples) was carried out. summary statistic is presented in Table 4.24 and 4.25.

t—values observed to be significant for all the twelve tasks for the two groups of Visually Impaired and for only 6 out of 12 tasks for the two groups of Sighted children.

To test the difference between the means of High and Low intelligence Visually Impaired children and High and Low Intelligence Sighted children for the twelve tasks on the number of critical features used, a t—test (independent means) was carried out. t—values observed from table 4.26 and 4.27 were significant for ten out of twelve tasks for the Visually Impaired and for only three out of twelve tasks for the Sighted groups.

TABLE : 4.24

T-VALUES FOR DIFFERENCE BETWEEN MEANS ON NUMBER OF FEATURES EMPLOYED IN EACH TASK BY HIGH AND LOW INTELLIGENCE VISUALLY IMPAIRED

S.NO.	PROBLEM TASK	GROUP	MEAN	SD	df	t-VALUE
1	2	3	4	5	6	7
1.	MATHS I	HIGH VISUALLY IMPAIRED	13.42	4.66	36	5.88**
		LOW VISUALLY IMPAIRED	5.74	3.11		
2.	MATHS II	HIGH VISUALLY IMPAIRED	11.16	2.81	36	4.88**
		LOW VISUALLY IMPAIRED	5.95	3.70		
3.	PATTERN MATCHING I	HIGH VISUALLY IMPAIRED	10.74	2.72	36	5.10**
		LOW VISUALLY IMPAIRED	8.53	3.90		
4.	PATTERN MATCHING II	HIGH VISUALLY IMPAIRED	16.80	5.63	36	6.48**
		LOW VISUALLY IMPAIRED	7.42	2.99		
5.	PUZZLE I	HIGH VISUALLY IMPAIRED	12.32	5.91	36	5.36**
		LOW VISUALLY IMPAIRED	4.53	2.22		
6.	PUZZLE II	HIGH VISUALLY IMPAIRED	9.79	4.94	36	2.63**
		LOW VISUALLY IMPAIRED	6.42	2.694		

1	2	3	4	5	6	7
7.	REASONING I	HIGH VISUALLY IMPAIRED	8.10	2.38	36	4.97**
		LOW VISUALLY IMPAIRED	4.58	1.98		
8.	REASONING II	HIGH VISUALLY IMPAIRED	6.52	1.26	36	4.12**
		LOW VISUALLY IMPAIRED	4.16	2.17		
9.	CIRCLE FORMATION I	HIGH VISUALLY IMPAIRED	13.74	6.51	36	5.10**
		LOW VISUALLY IMPAIRED	5.63	2.48		
10.	TRAIANGLE FORMATION II	HIGH VISUALLY IMPAIRED	11.00	4.95	36	2.83**
		LOW USUALLY IMPAIRED	5.16	2.57		
11.	ANIMAL RECOGNITION I	HIGH VISUALLY IMPAIRED	8.95	196	36	2.83**
		LOW VISUALLY IMPAIRED	6.74	2.74		
12.	ANIMAL RECOGNITION II	HIGH VISUALLY IMPAIRED	8.58	1.77	36.	2.25
		LOW VISUALLY IMPAIRED	7.00	2.50		

* Sig. at .05 level.

** Sig. at .01 level.

TABLE : 4.25

T-VALUEB FOR DIFFERENCE BETWEEN MEANS ON NUMBER OF FEATURES EMPLOYED IN EACH TASK BY HIGH AND LOW INTELLIGENCE SIGHTED

S.NO.	PROBLEM TASK	GROUP	MEAN	SD	df	t-VALUE
1	2	3	4	5	6	7
1.	MATHS	HIGH SIGHTED	14.9643	3.437	54	9.09**
		LOW SIGHTED	7.25	2.888		
2.	MATHS II	HIGH SIGHTED	10.4286	1.773	54	1.21
		LOW SIGHTED	9.3929	4.184		
3.	PATTERN MATCHING I	HIGH SIGHTED	9.57	1.87	54	3.24**
		LOW SIGHTED	7.61	2.601		
4.	PATTERN MATCHING II	HIGH SIGHTED	11.32	2.09	54	2.50**
		LOW SIGHTED	6.73	3.51		
5.	PUZZLE I	HIGH SIGHTED	10.32	12.041	54	1.52
		LOW SIGHTED	6.73	2.727		
6.	PUZZLE II	HIGH SIGHTED	8.857	1.976	54	96
		LOW SIGHTED	8.107	3.655		
7.	REASONING I	HIGH SIGHTED	6.57	1.59	54	-1.49
		LOW SIGHTED	7.43	2.60		
8.	REASONING II	HIGH SIGHTED	6.07	1.303	54	1.15
		LOW SIGHTED	5.46	2.472		
9.	CIRCLE FORMATION I	HIGH SIGHTED	9.257.46	2.303	54	2.57**
		LOW SIGHTED	7.46	2.861		

(Contd...)

1	2	3	4	5	6	7
10.	TRAIANGLE FORMATION II	HIGH SIGHTED	7.89	1.548	54	1.30
		LOW SIGHTED	7.07	2.968		
11.	ANIMAL RECOGNITION I	HIGH SIGHTED	10.19	2.138	54	3.15**
		LOW SIGHTED	8.78	2.510		
12.	ANIMAL RECOGNITION II	HIGH SIGHTED	9.179	2.278	54	2.00*
		LOW SIGHTED	7.857	2.663		

* Sig. at .05 Level.

** Sig. at .01 Level.

TABLE : 4.26

T-VALUES FOR DIFFERENCE BETWEEN MEANS ON NUMBER OF CRITICAL FEATURES EMPLOYED IN EACH TASK BY HIGH AND LOW VISUALLY IMPAIRED

S.NO.	PROBLEM TASK	GROUP	MEAN	SD	df	t-VALUE
1	2	3	4	5	6	7
1.	MATHS 1	HIGH VISUALLY IMPAIRED	6.42	2.34	36	4.67**
		LOW VISUALLY IMPAIRED	3.21	1.87		
2.	MATHS II	HIGH VISUALLY IMPAIRED	5.05	1.68	36	2.89**
		LOW VISUALLY IMPAIRED	3.16	2.31		
3.	PATTERN MATCHING I	HIGH VISUALLY IMPAIRED	6.26	1.82	36	1.07
		LOW VISUALLY IMPAIRED	5.42	2.89		

(Contd...)

1	2	3	4	5	6	7
4.	PATTERN MATCHING II	HIGH VISUALLY IMPAIRED	8.16	2.609	36	3.95**
		LOW VISUALLY IMPAIRED	5.05	2.223		
5.	PUZZLE I	HIGH VISUALLY IMPAIRED	4.947	2.297	36	3.42*
		LOW VISUALLY IMPAIRED	2.737	1.628		
6.	PUZZLE II	HIGH VISUALLY IMPAIRED	5.473	3.025	36	11.99*
		LOW VISUALLY IMPAIRED	3.789	2.097		
7.	REASONING I	HIGH VISUALLY IMPAIRED	4.74	1.195	36	4.34**
		LOW VISUALLY IMPAIRED	2.89	1.41		
8.	REASONING II	HIGH VISUALLY IMPAIRED	4.32	1.057	36	3.39**
		LOW VISUALLY IMPAIRED	2.79	1.653		
9.	CIRCLE FORMATION I	HIGH VISUALLY IMPAIRED	5.79	1.93	36	5.01**
		LOW VISUALLY IMPAIRED	2.95	1.54		
10.	TRAIANGLE FORMATION II	HIGH VISUALLY IMPAIRED	4.8	2.10	36	3.44**
		LOW VISUALLY IMPAIRED	92.63	1.95		

(Contd…)

1	2	3	4	5	6	7
11.	ANIMAL RECOGNITION I000	HIGH VISUALLY IMPAIRED	7.16	2.01	36	2.89**
		LOW VISUALLY IMPAIRED	5.37	1.80		
12.	ANIMAL RECOGNITION II	HIGH VISUALLY IMPAIRED	6.42	2.24	36	1.64
		LOW VISUALLY IMPAIRED	5.37	1.67		

* Sig. at .05 level.

** Sig. at .01 Level.

TABLE 4.27

T-VALUES FOR DIFFERENCE BETWEEN MEANS ON NUMBER OF CRITICAL FEATURES EMPLOYED) IN EACH TASK BY HIGH AND LOW INTELLIGENCE SIGHTED GROUP

S.NO.	PROBLEM TASK	GROUP	MEAN	SD	df	t-VALUE
1	2	3	4	5	6	7
1.	MATHS	HIGH SIGHTED	7.82	2.0	54	5.34**
		LOW SIGHTED	4.68	22.37		
2.	MATHS II	HIGH SIGHTED	5.71	1.76	54	.18
		LOW SIGHTED	5.61	2.66		
3.	PATTERN MATCHING I	HIGH SIGHTED	6.00	1.72	54	2.62**
		LOW SIGHTED	4.54	2.13		
4.	PATTERN MATCHING II	HIGH SIGHTED	6.93	1.84	54	.68
		LOW SIGHTED	6.43	3.44		

(Contd...)

1	2	3	4	5	6	7
5.	PUZZLE I	HIGH SIGHTED	5.53	4.53	54.	.93
		LOW SIGHTED	4.11	2.06		
6.	PUZZLE II	HIGH SIGHTED	4.53	1.14	54	-.47
		LOW SIGHTED	4.78	2.558		
7.	REASONING I	HIGH SIGHTED	4.11	1.37	54	-.94
		LOW SIGHTED	6.36	12.553		
8.	REASONING II	HIGH SIGHTED	4.00	1.19	54	1.88
	LOW SIGHTED		3.18	1.98		
9.	CIRCLE FORMATION I	HIGH SIGHTED	5.71	1.99	54	1.94
		LOW SIGHTED	4.64	72.129		
10.	TRAIANGLE FORMATION II	HIGH SIGHTED	4.46	.999	54	.85
		LOW SIGHTED	4.07	2.227		
11.	ANIMAL RECOGNITION I	HIGH SIGHTED	6.93	1.864	54	2.07*
		LOW SIGHTED	5.11	2.48		
12.	ANIMAL RECOGNITION II	HIGH SIGHTED	6.36	2.198	54	1.12
		LOW SIGHTED	5.68	2.326		

* Sig. at .05 Level.

** Sig. at .01 Level.

On reference to table number 4.17 to 4.22, Intelligence as a main effect on the time taken in training was significant for the tasks Maths I (F = 143.214, df 1,90, p < .01); Pattern Matching (F = 123.737, df = 1,90, P < .01); Balance—Scale (F = 123.784, df = 1,90, P < .01); Reasoning (F = 89.153, df = 1,90, P < .01); Circle Formation (F =90.03, df = 1,90, p < .01); Animal Recognition (F = 109.781, df = 1,90, p < .01). Fig 4.15, presents mean values for two Visually Impaired groups and two Sighted groups of High and Low intelligence.

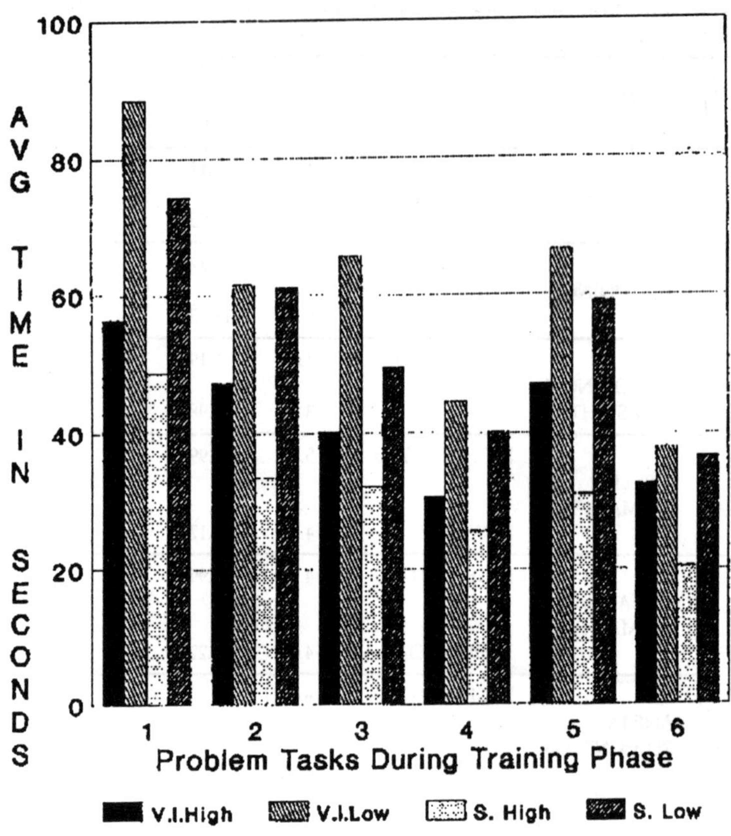

Fig. 4.15 Average Time taken for Training High and Low Intelligence Subjects.

Media of Presentation

The training phase was divided in two parts. In the first main part the two Visually Impaired groups (High and Low in intelligence) were trained through the braille script for six tasks and the two groups of the sighted subjects (High and Low in intelligence) were trained through print script. Comparisons were made between these groups after the training in the testing phase for twelve tasks.

The second part of the training consisted of training ten Visually Impaired subjects and ten Sighted subjects of high intelligence through the audio medium. Comparisons were then made between this Visually Impaired group and high intelligence Visually Impaired group trained through braille script for all the twelve tasks in the testing phase and also between the Sighted group trained through audio and print media.

Table 4.28-4.39 present summary ANOVA for 2x2 factorial design with vision status at two levels (Visually Impaired and Sighted) and Media of Presentation at two levels (Braille/Print and Audio) for No. of words. Main effect of vision stAtus was found to be significant for the Problem Tasks, Pattern Matching I, Pattern Matching II, Puzzle I and Puzzle II, Reasoning I, Reasoning II, Circle Formation, Animal Recognition I and Animal Recognition II, i.e. in 9 out of 12 tasks.

TABLE : 4.28

SUMMARY ANOVA WITH MEDIA OF PRESENTATION (2 LEVELS) ANDVISION STATUS (2 LEVELS) ON NUMBER OF WORDS EMPLOYED IN MATHS I

SOURCES OF VARIATION	SUM OF SQUARES	dF	M Square	F
VISION STATUS (VISUALLY IMPAIRED AND SIGHTED)	14063.36	1	14063.36	1.672
MEDIA OF PRESENTATION (BRAILLE/PRINT ANDAUDIO)	10154.16	1	10154.16	1.207
TWO WAY INTERACTION (VISION STATUS X MEDIA OF PRESENTATION	1855.593	1	1855.593	.221
RESIDUAL	529926.255	63	8411.528	
TOTAL	**558320.299**	**66**	**8459.398**	

TABLE : 4.29

SUMMARY ANOVA WITH MEDIA OF PRESENTATION (2 LEVELS) AND VISION STATUS (2 LEVELS) ON NUM~ER OF WORDS EMPLOYED IN MATHS II

SOURCES OF VARIATION	SUM OF SQUARES	dF	M Square	F
VISION STATUS (VISUALLY IMPAIRED AND SIGHTED)	659.259	1	659.259	.205
MEDIA OF PRESENTATION (BRAILLE/PRINT ANDAUDIO)	5563.340	1	5563.640	1.731
TWO WAY INTERACTION (VISION STATUS X MEDIA OF PRESENTATION	8020.472	1	8020.472	2.495
RESIDUAL	202529.376	63	3214.752	
TOTAL	**216480.119**	**66**	**3280.002**	

TABLE : 4.30

SUMMARY ANOVA WITH MEDIA OF PRESENTATION (2 LEVELS) AND VISION STATUS (2 LEVELS) ON NUMBER OF WORDS EMPLOYED IN PATTERN MATCHING I

SOURCES OF VARIATION	SUM OF SQUARES	dF	N Square	F
VISION STATUS (VISUALLY IMPAIRED AND SIGHTED)	1220.837	1	1220.837	5.948*
MEDIA OF PRESENTATION (BRAILLE/PRINT ANDAUDIO)	243.619	1	243.619	1.187
TWO WAY INTERACTION (VISION STATUS X MEDIA OF PRESENTATION	62.764	1	62.764	.306
RESIDUAL	12931.135	63	205.256	
TOTAL	**14372.687**	**66**	**217.768**	

* Sig. at .05 level.

TABLE : 4.31

SUMMARY ANOVA WITH MEDIA OF. PRESENTATION (2 LEVELS) AND VISION STATUS (2 LEVELS) ON NUMBER OF WORDS EMPLOYEDIN PATTERN MATCHING II

SOURCES OF VARIATION	SUM OF SQUARES	dF	N Square	F
VISION STATUS (VISUALLY IMPAIRED AND SIGHTED)	21646.545	1	21646.545	6.701**
MEDIA OF PRESENTATION (BRAILLE/PRINT AND AUDIO)	433.695	1	433.695	.134
TWO WAY INTERACTION (VISION STATUS X MEDIA OF PRESENTATION	1827.113	1	1827.113	.566
RESIDUAL	203515.828	63	3230.410	
TOTAL	**227051.045**	**66**	**3440.167**	

** Sig. at .01 level.

TABLE : 4.32

SUMMARY ANOVA WITH MEDIA OF PRESENTATION (2 LEVELS) AND VISION STATUS (2 LEVELS) ON NUMBER OF WORDS EMPLOYED IN PUZZLE I

SOURCES OF VARIATION	SUM OF SQUARES	dF	M Square	F
VISION STATUS (VISUALLY IMPAIRED AND SIGHTED)	53067.010	1	53067.010	22.237**
MEDIA OF PRESENTATION (BRAILLE/PRINT AND AUDIO)	909.043	1	909.043	.381
TWO WAY INTERACTION (VISION STATUS X MEDIA OF PRESENTATION	297.556	1	297.556	.125
RESIDUAL	150347.212	63	2386.464	
TOTAL	**203808.17**	**66**	**3088.003**	

** Sig. at .01 level.

TABLE : 4.33

SUMMARY ANOVA WITH MEDIA OF PRESENTATION (2 LEVELS) ANDVISION STATUS (2 LEVELS) ON NUMBER OF WORDS EMPLOYED IN PUZZLE II

SOURCES OF VARIATION	SUM OF SQUARES	dF	M Square	F
VISION STATUS (VISUALLY IMPAIRED AND SIGHTED)	30262.000	1	30262.000	123.858**
MEDIA OF PRESENTATION (BRAILLE/PRINT AND AUDIO)	5.005	1	5.005	.002
TWO WAY INTERACTION (VISION STATUS X MEDIA OF PRESENTATION	17.039	3.	17.039	.008
RESIDUAL	137575.565	63	2183.739	
TOTAL	**168028.776**	**66**	**2545.891**	

** Sig. at .01 level.

TABLE 4.34

SUMMARY ANOVA WITH MEDIA OF IRESENTATION (2 LEVELS) AND VISION STATUS (2 LEVELS) ON NUMBER OF WORDS EMPLOYED IN REASONING I

SOURCES OF VARIATION	SUM OF SQUARES	dF	M Square	F
VISION STATUS (VISUALLY IMPAIRED AND SIGHTED)	3846.824	1	3846.824	6.101*
MEDIA OF PRESENTATION (BRAILLE/PRINT AND AUDIO)	517.282	1	517.282	.820
TWO WAY INTERACTION (VISION STATUS X MEDIA OF PRESENTATION	5.168	1	5.168	.008
RESIDUAL	39725.633	63	630.566	
TOTAL	**44380.746**	**66**	**672.436**	

* Sig. at .05 level.

TABLE : 4.35

5U304ARY ANOVA WITH MEDIA OF PRESENTATION (2 LEVELS)AND VISION STATUS (2 LEVELS) ON NUMBER OFWORDS ENPLOYEDIN REASONING II

SOURCES OF VARIATION	SUM OF SQUARES	dF	M Square	F
VISION STATUS (VISUALLY IMPAIRED AND SIGHTED)	2365.045	1	2365.045	7.473**
MEDIA OF PRESENTATION (BRAILLE/PRINT AND AUDIO)	132.448	1	132.448	.418
TWO WAY INTERACTION (VISION STATUS X MEDIAOF PRESENTATION	76.683	1	76.683	.242
RESIDUAL	19939.094	63	316.494	
TOTAL	**22632.716**	**66**	**342.920**	

** Sig. at .01 level.

TABLE : 4.36

SUMMARY ANOVA WITH MEDIA OF PRESENTATION (2 LEVELS) AND VISION STATUS (2 LEVELS) ON NUMBER OF WORDS EMPLOYED IN CIRCLE FORMATION

SOURCES OF VARIATION	SUM OF SQUARES	dF	M Square	F
VISION STATUS (VISUALLY IMPAIRED AND SIGHTED)	16821.971	1	16821.971	12.188**
MEDIA OF PRESENTATION (BRAILLE/PRINT ANDAUDIO)	5179.722	1	5179.722	3.753*
TWO WAY INTERACTION (VISION STATUS X MEDIAOF PRESENTATION	115.700	1	115.700	.084
RESIDUAL	86949.705	63	1380.154	
TOTAL	**107576.627**	**66**	**1629.949**	

* Sig. at .05 level.

** Sig. at .01 level.

TABLE : 4.37

SUMMARY ANOVA WITH MEDIA OF PRESENTATION (2 LEVELS) AND VISION STATUS (2 LEVELS) ON NUMBER OF WORDS EMPLOYED IN TRIANGLE FORMATION

SOURCES OF VARIATION	SUM OF SQUARES	dF	M Square	F
VISION STATUS (VISUALLY IMPAIRED AND SIGHTED)	4609.063	1	4609.063	.606
MEDIA OF PRESENTATION (BRAILLE/PRINT AND AUDIO)	1135.681	1	1135.681	.149
TWO WAY INTERACTION (VISION STATUS X MEDIA OF PRESENTATION	2600.750	1	2600.756	.342
RESIDUAL	478843.791	63	7600.695	
TOTAL	**486826.746**	**66**	**7376.163**	

TABLE 4.38

SUMMARY ANOVA WITH MEDIA OF PRESENTATION (2 LEVELS) AND VISION STATUS (2 LEVELS) ON NUMBER OF WORDS EMPLOYED IN ANIMAL RECOGNITION I

SOURCES OF VARIATION	SUM OF SQUARES	dF	M Square	F
VISION STATUS (VISUALLY IMPAIRED AND SIGHTED)	806.205	1	806.205	5.804*
MEDIA OF PRESENTATION (BRAILLE/PRINT AND AUDIO)	76.070	1	76.070	.548
TWO WAY INTERACTION (VISION STATUS X MEDIA OF PRESENTATION	8750.984	63	138.905	
RESIDUAL	13.556	1	13.556	.098
TOTAL	**9697.910**	**66**	**146.938**	

* Sig. at .05 level.

TABLE : 4.39

SUMMARY ANOVA WITH MEDIA OF PRESENTATION (2 LEVELS) AND VISION STATUS (2 LEVELS) ON NUMBER OF WORDS EMPLOYED IN ANIMAL RECOGNITION II

SOURCES OF VARIATION	SUM OF SQUARES	dF	M Square	F
VISION STATUS (VISUALLY IMPAIRED AND SIGHTED)	1253.254	1	1253.254	23.564**
MEDIA OF PRESENTATION (BRAILLE/PRINT AND AUDIO)	34.056	1	34.056	.640
TWO WAY INTERACTION (VISION STATUS X MEDIA OF PRESENTATION	80.255	1	.80.255	1.509
RESIDUAL	3350.658	63	53.185	
TOTAL	**4765.194**	**66**	**72.200**	

** Sig at .01 level.

Main effect of Media of Presentation (Braille/Print and Audio) was significant for the task Circle Formation (F = 3.75, df = 1,90, P .05) only.

Interaction effect (Vision Status x Media of Presentation) was found not to be significant in any task.

The Visually Impaired children used larger number of rules in writinq the production systems for eleven tasks as a function of media of presentation. Fig 4.16 and 4.17 show the number of rules used for each problem task and also percentage of Visually Impaired subjects using more than one rule.

Fig.4.18 given below shows the difference in the percentage of sighted subjects using more than one rule as a function of media presentation. Fig.4.19 given below shows number of rules used by the Sighted subjects for each problem task as a function of media of presentation.

To test the difference between the means for number of features of those trained by audio medium and those trained by braille medium in the Visually Impaired group for 12 tasks, t—test (independent samples) was carried out.

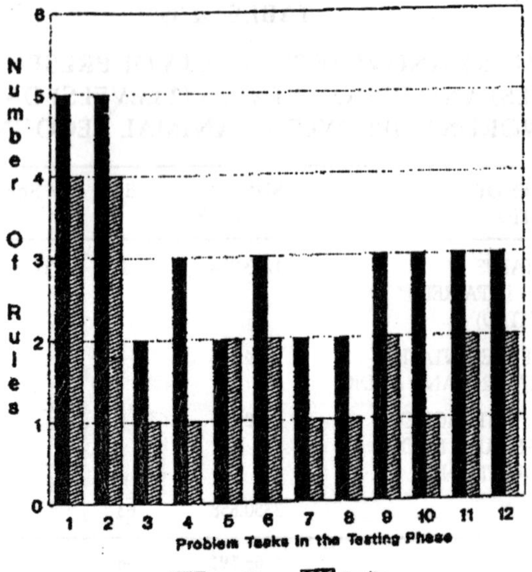

Fig. 4.16 No. of Rules used by Visually Impaired Trained by Braille/Audio

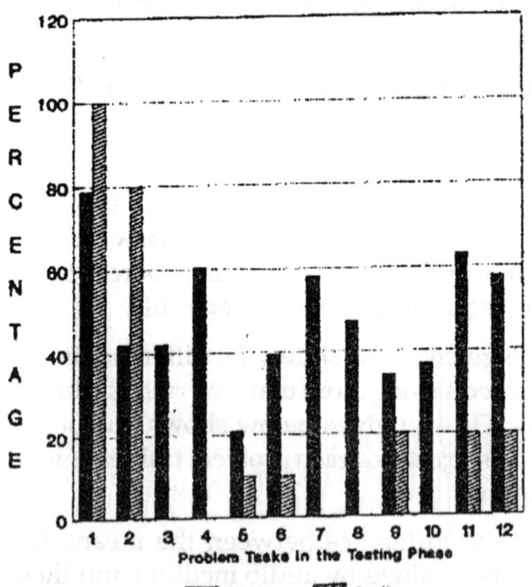

Fig. 4.17 % of Visually Impaired more than 1 rule trained by braille/Audio

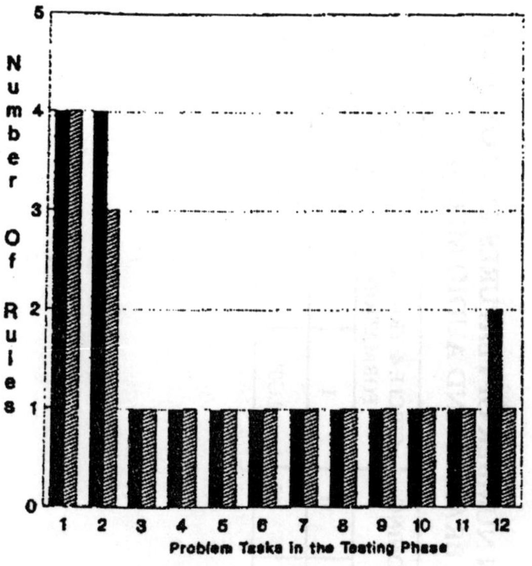

Fig. 4.18 No. of Rules used by Sighted trained by print/Audio

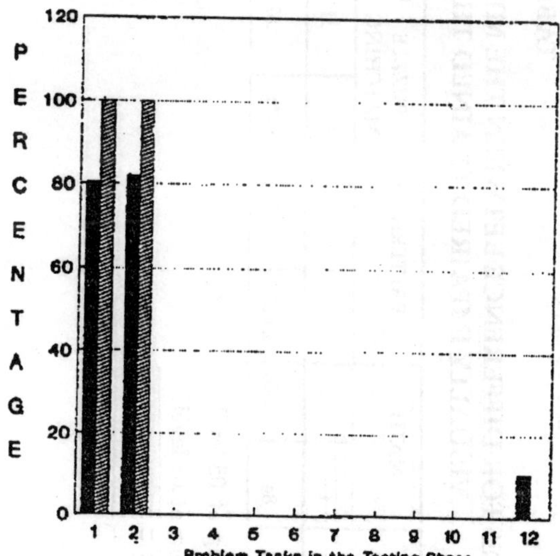

Fig. 4.19 % of Sighted using more than 1 rule trained by print/Audio

t—values observed to be significant for the tasks Pattern Matching I, Parking Puzzle, Circle Formation are presented in Table 4.40.

TABLE : 4.40

VALUES FOR DIFFERENCE BETWEEN THE MEANS ON NUMBER OF FEATURES EMPLOYED BY VISUALLY IMPAIRED TRAINED THROUGH BRAILLE AND AUDIO MEDIA

TASKS	MATH		PATTERN		PUZZLE MATCHING		REASONING		CIRCLE & TRIANGLE FORMATION		ANIMAL RECOGNITION	
	I	II	I	II	I	II	I	II	I	II	I	II
t-VALUES	84	1.06	2.00*	.79	2.61**	.87	–1.56	.67	–2.O0*	–.51	–.33	–.56

* Sig. at .05 level.

** Sig. at .01 level.

t—values observed to be significant for .the Sighte~1 population when trained through audio or print media for no. of features on problem tasks Maths II ($t = 2.19$, $df = 27$, $p < .05$), Pattern Matching I ($t = 2.19$, $df = 27$, $P < .05$), Puzzle I ($t = 2.60$, ~$df = 27$, $P < .05$), Puzzle II ($t = 2.48$, $df = 27$, $P < .05$), Reasoning I ($t = 2.53$, df 27, $P < .05$), Reasoning II ($t = 5.10$, $df = 27$, $P < .01$), Triangle Formation ($t = 3.43$, $df = 27$, $P < .01$).

TABLE : 4.41

LUES FOR DIFFERENCE BETWEEN THE MEANS ON NUMBER OF CRITICAL FEATURES EMPLOYED BY VISUALLY IMPAIRED TRAINED THROUGH BRAILLE AND AUDIO MEDIA

TASKS	MATH		PATTERN MATCHING		PUZZLE		REASONING		CIRCLE & TRIANGLE FORMATION		ANIMAL RECOGNITION	
	I	II	I	II	I	II	I	II	I	II	I	II
t-VALUES	-1.11	-.62	-2.93**	-.57	.-1.81	.54	-2.53*	-2.19*	-2.31*	-.52	-.60	-.65

* Sig. at .05 level.

** Sig. at .01 level.

Table 4.41 shows the Visually Impaired children trained through braille medium differed from Visually Impaired children trained through audio medium on number of critical features in the Tasks Pattern Matching I ($t = 2.93$, $df = 27$, $P < .01$), Reasoning I (t 2.53, $df = 27$, $P < .05$), Reasoning II ($t = 2.19$, $df = 27$, $p < .05$) and Circle Formation ($t = 2.31$, $df = 27$, $P < .05$).

Sighted children trained through audio medium did not differ from Sighted children trained through print on number of critical features for any problem tasks.

Findings

1. Visually Impaired group used more words to generate production systems in the testing phase for Pattern Matching I, Parking Puzzle, and Animal Recognition I and 1E i.e. in four out of twelve tasks. The null hypothesis of no difference between the two groups was rejected for the four tasks given above but accepted for all the other tasks.
2. The high intelligence group differed significantly from low intelligence group on number of words used in generating protocols in eleven out of twelve tasks. Only with respect to Pattern Matching II there was no difference found. The null hypothesis of no difference was rejected for eleven tasks but accepted for one task.
3. The interaction effect between Vision status and Intelligence was significant for seven out of twelve tasks for number of words.
4. Visually Impaired children generally used more words than Sighted children in generating production rules in nine out of twelve tasks though, as mentioned, the difference was significant in only 4 tasks.
5. The low intelligence group of Visually Impaired used less words to generate production systems for eleven out of twelve tasks as compared to high intelligence Visually Impaired group.

6. The low intelligence group of Sighted children used less words to generate production systems for nine out of twelve tasks as compared to high intelligence Sighted group.
7. The word rate/unit of time was lower in the Visually Impaired sample as compared to the Sighted sample.
8. The Visually Impaired children used larger number rules than Sighted children for generating production systems for all the twelve tasks.
9. The Visually Impaired children trained through braille script used more rules to write production systems in eleven out of twelve tasks compared to Visually Impaired, trained through audio mode.
10. Difference was found in the sighted children for number of rules in only two tasks, as a functton of media of presentation.
11. Visually Impaired did not differ from Sighted on quality of production rules for eleven out of twelve tasks. Only in respect to Triangle Formation the quality of production rules was better for the Sighted group. Thus, the null hypothesis that there will be no significant difference between the Visually Impaired group and the Sighted group was accepted for eleven tasks but rejected for one task.
12. No difference between Visually Impaired and sighted groups was observed in number of features written, in the production rules for eleven out of twelve tasks. Only with respect to Animal Recognition I, the sighted children differed from the Visually Impaired in writing more features. Thus, the null hypothesis that there will be no difference in Visually Impaired and Sighted group on number of features used in writing production systems, was accepted for eleven tasks but rejected for one task.

13. The high and low intelligence Visually Impaired groups differed significantly on number of features used in writing production rules in all the twelve tasks, where as, the Sighted children differed on number of features written in the production rules in only five out of twelve tasks. Both in the Visually Impaired sighted group the high intelligence wrote more features. Thus, the null hypothesis, that, there will be no difference between high and low intelligence Visually Impaired on number of features used was rejected for all the tasks, but the null hypothesis, that, there will be no difference between the high and low intelligence Sighted children was rejected for five tasks but accepted for seven tasks.

14. Media of presentation (braille/audio) did not affect number of features used by the Visually Impaired, in generating of production systems in nine out of twelve tasks. The difference was observed in only three tasks. In Pattern *Matching* I and Parking puzzle, more features resulted from training, when it was given through audio mode and in circle formation more features were generated when training was given through the braille script. Thus, the null hypothesis, that, there will be no difference between the high intelligence Visually Impaired trained through braille arid high intelligence Visually Impaired trained through audio on number of features used was rejected for three tasks but accepted for nine tasks.

15. sighted children used more features in writing production systems when trained through print script in tasks like Maths II, Pattern Matching I, but in tasks like Puzzle I and II, Reasoning I and II and Triangle formation they wrote more features when trained through the audio mode. Thus, the null hypothesis, that, there will be no difference between high and low intelligence Sighted groups trained through print script and high intelligence Sighted trained through audio mode was rejected for seven tasks but accepted for five tasks.

16. No significant difference was observed between the Visually Impaired and Sighted children in number of critical features used in the production rules generated during the testing phase in. ten out of twelve tasks. Only, in the tasks Maths I and II the sighted children significantly wrote more critical features. Therefore, the null hypothesis, that, there will be no difference between the visually impaired and sighted children on number of critical features used was accepted for ten tasks but rejected for two tasks.

17. Intelligence affected the No. of critical features used in production rules in the Visually Impaired group for ten out of twelve problem tasks with the high intelligence Visually Impaired group writing more critical features than low intelligence Visually Impaired group. In the Sighted group, intelligence affected number of critical features written in only three tasks in which the high intelligence Sighted group wrote more critical features than low intelligence Sighted group. Thus, the null hypothesis, that, there will be rio difference between high and low intelligence Visually Impaired children in number of critical features was rejected for ten tasks but accepted for two tasks, whereas, the null hypothesis, that there will be no difference between the high and low intelligence Sighted children on number of critical features was rejected for three tasks and accepted for nine tasks.

18. Visually Impaired children trained thrQugh audio, mode used more critical features in the production rules for tasks Pattern Matching I, Reasoning I and II and Circle Formation. No such difference, as a function, of media of presentation was found for the Sighted children. The null hypothesis, that, there will be no difference between Visually Impaired trained through braille and Visually Impaired trained audio mode on number of critical features used was rejected for four tasks but accepted for eight tasks. The null hypothesis, that, there will be no difference between Sighted group

trained through print script and Sighted group trained through audio mode mode on critical features used was accepted for all tasks.

19. The Visually Impaired children took more time than Sighted children in acquiring training in the use of production rules for all the six tasks of the training phase. Thus the Null hypothesis, that, there will be no significant difference in the time taken during training between the Visually Impaired and Sighted group was rejected for all the tasks.

20. The low intelligence Visually Impaired and Sighted children took more time in learning production systems than the high intelligence Visually Impaired and Sighted group. Thus, the null hypothesis, that, there will be no difference between 1.iigh and low intelligence groups in time taken for training was rejected for all the tasks.

21. The Visually Impaired children differed from the sighted group on time taken to solve all the problem tasks in the testing phase. Thus, the null hypothesis, that, there will be no significant difference between the Visually Impaired and Sighted group in time taken to solve the problems was rejected for all the tasks.

Conclusions

1. The cognitive architecture of the Visually Impaired, according to the findings obtained, in the framework of present research, is slower in functioning than that of the Sighted controls.

2. Visually Impaired took significantly more time to acquire knowledge or learn production rules related to six tasks in the training phase as compared to the Sighted controls.

3. Visually Impaired took significantly more time to solve all the tasks in the testing phase as compared to their Sighted controls. It was observed that many of the low

intelligence Visually Impaired abandoned the problem in between after taking a long time over it. Few of the low intelligence Sighted children also abandoned the problem solving.

4. The programming of knowledge or collapsing the productions into one production is evident in the Sighted sample only.

5. Visually Impaired, though slow in learning production rules, can generalize this rule-based logical thinking to other similar but different problems as becomes evident in the quality of rules given by the Visually Impaired.

6. Visually Impaired children have to be highly intelligent to grasp and retrieve knowledge from the production rules to be applied in subsequent problem solving situation, supported by the finding that the high intelligent Visually Impaired children significantly used more features and critical features than their low intelligent counterparts in all the twelve tasks.

7. Media of Presentation, during the training phase affects the comprehension and application of that knowledge only in certain tasks, in the Visually, Impaired (for number of features employed—three out of twelve tasks, for number of critical feature employed□f our out of twelve tasks). In the Sighted controls the difference was significant in six out of twelve tasks for number of features, but for number of critical features employed, the difference was not significant for any task.

8. Media of presentation affected the number of rules used by the Visually Impaired. They used more production rules to solve eleven out of twelve tasks when trained through braille mode. This difference, as a result of media of presentation was observed in only two out of twelve tasks for the Sighted controls.

5

DISCUSSION, LIMITATIONS AND SUGGESTIONS FOR FURTHER RESEARCH

Discussions

Based on the findings, the following broad conclusions can now be drawn:

1. The cognitive architecture of the Visually Impaired, according to the findings obtained in the framework of present research, is slower in functioning than that of the Sighted controls. Support for the above is derived from the following findings:

   (a) *Word rate employed:* Visually impaired children employed lower word rate/unit of time as compared to that employed by the sighted controls.

   (b) *Organization of Language:* Visually Impaired children used more words than the Sighted group. The Sighted organized their rules around fewer words.

2. The low intelligent in the Sighted and Visually Impaired sample used lesser words than the high intelligent. This difference was because of the fact that, the low intelligence group abandoned the problem half way and the number of words used by them were less than the high intelligence group.

3. Visually Impaired took significantly more time to acquire knowledge or learn production rules related to six tasks in the training phases as compared to the Sighted controls.

4. Visually Impaired took significantly more time to solve all the tasks in the testing phase as compared to the Sighted controls. It was observed that many of the low intelligent Visually Impaired abandoned the problem in between after taking a long time over it. Few of the low intelligent Sighted children also abandoned the problem solving. Both the above findings support once again, the slowness of functioning of the cognitive architecture of the Visually Impaired.

5. The programming of knowledge or collapsing the productions into one production is evident in the Sighted sample only, supported by the finding that the Sighted employ just one rule to solve nine out of twelve tasks. While the Visually Impaired employ more than one rule in all the tasks which can be taken to support discrete operations, serially organized by the Visually Impaired children.

6. Visually Impaired, though slow in learning production rules, can generalize this rule based logical thinking to other similar but different problems as becomes evident in the quality of rules given by the Visually Impaired. There was no significant difference found between the Visually Impaired and Sighted children in eleven out of twelve tasks.

7. Visually Impaired children have to be highly intelligent to grasp and retrieve knowledge from the production

rules to be applied in subsequent problem solving situation, supported by the finding that the high intelligence Visually Impaired significantly used more features and critical features than their low intelligence counterparts in all the twelve tasks. This difference between the high and low intelligence Sighted children was found in only 6 out of 12 tasks for number of features and in 3 out of 12 tasks for number of critical features.

8. Media of Presentation, during the training phase affects the comprehension and application of that knowledge only in certain tasks in the Visually Impaired, supported by the finding that there was a significant difference in only three out of twelve tasks for number of features employed and in only four out of twelve tasks in number of critical features employed. In the Sighted controls the difference was significant in six out of twelve tasks for number of features, but for number of critical features used, the difference was not significant for any task.

9. Media of presentation affected the number of rules used by the Visually Impaired. They used more production rules to solve eleven out of twelve tasks when trained through braille mode. This difference, as a result of media of presentation was observed in only 2 out of 12 tasks for the sighted controls.

The general picture that one builds up from the above conclusions is that the Visually Impaired children are having a slower functioning cognitive architecture. This is supported by the fact that they are slower in learning, grasping, organizing and then converging information than their sighted counterparts. The information intake is slower and of a different order than as observed in the Sighted children. The overall organization or cognitive plasticity, nevertheless, does not affect the quality of the rules they produce as reflected in number of features and critical features they use as compared to the Sighted.

The Visually Impaired children, it has been shown by the studies mentioned later, code information in terms of successive inputs and serial unlike the Sighted population who get a global picture of the problem space employing both successive and simultaneous processing. If the Visually Impaired are given longer time to integrate and code information from sense modalities other than vision, their accuracy improves to that of the level of the Sighted in terms of the units of knowledge they can retrieve from the knowledge acquired during the training phase. Intelligence seems to affect the Visually Impaired not only in acquiring knowledge but also in retrieving it. Many low intelligent subjects in both the samples tended to abandon a problem in between even after the training. The relation between intelligence and solving of difficult problems has been studied by Dorner Dietrich and Kreuzig, Heinz W. (1983). Contrary to the above findings they found a low correlation between difficult problems (Tangram puzzles, Oranization tasks, Text interpretation tasks) with measures of intelligence. They suggested that operative abilities and subjective estimates of competence play an essential role in problem solving activities but not in those processes involved in solving items on intelligence tests. Spilabury, Georgina, Stankov, Lazar and Roberts, Richards (1990) explored the relationship between intelligence and working memory load in a verbal reasoning task, the 4 term series problem. They found that increasing the working memory demand of this task increased the task's difficulty but did not increase its correlation with intelligence. Taking individual's deviation latent ability score which is independent of item difficulty, a high correlation was found with fluid intelligence. The research findings quoted are drawn from a Sighted sample. No study, relating intelligence to solving of various tasks by the Visually Impaired could be found.

The present study shows that the Visually Impaired children produced more critical features when trained through braille script. However, they could integrate rules better when trained through audio mode. The results, therefore, support, that in coding information serially for the Visually Impaired, braille is a more successful medium as oral presentation does not provide them with an environment to space their learning. The integration of knowledge, in terms of lesser number of rules used to solve the problem by the audio mode suggest a strategy of training with both the braille and audio medium.

The overall picture that emerges is supported by numerous studies. According to Anderson (1983), multiple neural centres extract different but overlapping information from visual signals. Mind, therefore, evolves by employing multiple overlapping systems to optimize various aspects of mental processing supporting the role of senses in achieving information. According to Bushnell (1981) "the ontogeny of intermodel relations is not a simple unitary process but is instead a many faceted one, the development of which is gradual, complex and interdependent with expertness and with developments." Millar (1981) concluded that sense modalities are neither separate nor unitary they are complementary and convergent.

Thus, when the visual system is impaired or completely non — functional, reliance on the other sensory systems increases. The results of the present research show, that, in the absence of sight, information intake presented through other medias is much more slower and difficult for the Visually Impaired. However, the research has also shown that loss of vision may slow the pace but doesn't prevent them from becoming equivalent to sighted (Millar, 1981), as reflected in the number of features and critical features they have used. Accdrding to Millar (1981) absence of active interaction is more detrimental than deprivation of vision in constructing sensory motor schema. Witkin and associates (1968) on the basis of their study on congenitally totally blind children, has said, that, to form impressions of objects as discrete and as structured through senses other than vision was possible but much more difficult.

Sally M. Bailes and Robert M. Lambert (1986) studying haptic form recognition tasks have concluded that sighted subjects are both faster and more accurate than adventitiously and congenitally blind and all the groups improve in accuracy as a function of interstimulus interval.

Anderson (1983) makes a distinction between declarative and procedural knowledge in his ACT framework. Declarative knowledge is represented in a propositional network. This is contrasted to Newell and Simon's suggestion that all knowledge, procedural or declarative, is represented in productions. Oswald, Hargit, Gadenne and Volker (1984) have analyzed the concept of declarative and procedural knowledge. They have stated that researchers in Artificial Intelligence argue that procedural knowledge can be converted into declarative knowledge and vice versa so that the distinction is merely a perspective. Psychologists also, according to them, refute the distinction between declarative and procedural knowledge arguing that people have direct access to products of their thoughts but not to their cognitive processes.

Whatever may be the case, the present research clearly shows that training intervention in terms of production rules can cover—up to a great extent any lag due to visual handicap in solving varied tasks related to the study. The features represented in the inputs, in terms of production rules, related to particular task, are features which are built or represented in the rules from the environment. With subsequent experience with the similar situations in the environment, salient features can be retrieved and applied. These features can make changes in the declarative content, whether permanent or temporary, would depend on the experience the subject has or practice they get in acquiring these features. Thus, a new skill can be acquired or a new task can be solved without prior knowledge. This can help the Visually Impaired to come at par with the sighted, provided they get enough time to comprehend the salient features from the rule—based knowledge, store it in the form of propositions (Anderson 1983) or productions (Newell and Simon 1972) in long-term memory and retrieve it when they require it to solve problems in the same domain as in which they were trained or instructed. Kolovsky, Hayes and Simon (1985) have concluded that intensive training in the rules, even in isolation from any problem setting or knowledge significantly decreases the difficulty of the problem.

Pirolli and Anderson (1984) developed ACT production-system model of recrusive programming and concluded that how—to instruction was better than conventional instruction.

J.R. Anderson and Reiser (1985) contrasted one group solving problems on their own with another group solving problems with the LISP tutor and concluded that the LISP tutor was more successful. The advantage of this kind of intelligent tutoring is their ability to facilitate the conversion of abstract declarative instruction into procedures by providing the instruction appropriately in context.

Voromin, V.M. (1985) have also discussed the effective stimulation of cognitive and communicative activity in students with severe visual impairment with the use of computer technology in physics and mathematics classes.

Breuer, Klaus and Kummer, Ruediger (1990) discussed computer managed simulations (CMSs) as a part of learning environments in which students use their knowledge in the generations of solutions to problems. This, according to them, improves the students' cognitive abilities or strategies in the realm of vocational education.

According to Anderson (1987) there can be a positive transfer between two skills or tasks provided the two skills involve the same production. The results of the present study, in terms of two levels of similar domain problem, did show a reduction of time on the second level of each problem domain during testing phase.

The two problems were different but covered the same domain and the subjects took lesser time to solve and state the related production rules. Transfer effects in productions have been shown by Singley and Anderson (1985) for text editing task.

Contentwise also (Thorndike, 1903) there were indications of positive transfer as the number of words used to write productions for the second level were lesser than the first level and the rules were shorter and more concise. This is supported by Kolers and Smythe, (1984).

In the Mathematics task the Visually Impaired took maximum time indicating interference from a strategy of mental calculation the Visually Impaired had evolved for themselves. Similar result was not found in the Sighted controls.

For Pattern Matching and Animal Recognition tasks, the visually impaired differed from the sighted coi~trols on number of parameters (number of words, number of features, time etc.).

Knowledge related to both the tasks engineered in rules could not overcome the role of vision in tasks like Pattern Matching and Animal Recognition. Witkin and associates (1968) have shown superiority of Sighted subjects on some tasks. Davidson (1976), Foulke (1964), Santin and Nesker (1977) have also concluded that Sighted children's mental images or concepts of objects, which are based on their visually directed experience of objects may not match those of blind children which are generated through touch, hearing etc. sense that provide inconsistent bits of information. These tasks may also be having a spatial perspective to them, which would affected the performance of the Visually Impaired.

Another obs.ervation mentioned earlier, arising from this study was, the larger number of rules the Visually Impaired used as compared to Sighted controls, who used one rule for most of the tasks except Mathematics. This indicates that Visually Impaired use a coding system based on successive inputs, whereas the Sighted have a global representation. The use of one rule by the Sighted group could be interpreted in terms of knowledge compilation process described by Anderson (1982,1983), that collapses sequences of productions into one production and therefore speeding up the solution of problems. Since the Sighted took less time to solve problems as compared to Visually Impaired, predicts the knowledge compilation process. This result can also be interpreted in terms of what Miller (1956) calls, chunking process. Newell and Rosenbloom (1981) have also applied the chunking process to productions.

The media of training whether audio or braille script did not affect learning and utilizing knowledge in solving various problems in the testing phase. In fact, for the Visually Impaired, braille script was quite successful as a medium of learning. Since, the serial organization of inputs by the Visually Impaired has been discussed, it further supports the advantage reading has over listening though results of studies done before have found orally presented material was much more effective than silent reading by the blind (Erikson and King, 1917; Biachoff, 1967; Bixler, 1963; Cobb, 1977; Daightery, 1974; Gore, 1969; Halten, 1976). Karrakar (1952) on the contrary, has emphasized the role of type of material to be comprehended supported by N.K. Rai (1987) who found significant difference between tactile and auditory medias, only for some classes and not for all. The result that audio presentation facilitates integrating of knowledge lends support to a strategy of training involving both the braille and oral media of training.

Limitations and Suggestions for Further Research

The present research aimed at studying features of cognitive architecture in the Visually Impaired. The findings implied a a slowness in the functioning of cognitive architecture of the Visually Impaired as compared to the sighted controls but not in the quality of acquired production rules. These findings highlight the necessity of providing visually Impaired children with information, step by step, using simple, systematic, serially organized and by symbolic logical methods presented through braille script or orally in the absence of visual modality. However, these information intake methods many not be easily available to the Visually Impaired.

Finding.are suggestive of extension of this research in the following directions:

1. There is a need to develop a strategy that programs knowledge related to various tasks to be solved i.e. intelligent tutoring system. The implementation of production rules, related to tasks in different domains, on computers, can teach a student to solve a class of problems the student isbeing asked to solve in the same way that the student should solve the problem (Anderson 1993). Since the Visually Impaired children get the information from other modalities which is segmentory and has to be integrated and also depends on the experience a Visually Impaired child has with the environment, it would be highly advantageous if they can get rich information, orally, in a set of rules, which run serially, are independent from each other, simple and flexible.

2. The study did not go into the analysis of analyzing the subjects' behavior in attributing specific problem solving behavior to specific rules. If the performance of the rules can be monitored, it will further help in designing computer—based programs for specific problems.

3. Error analysis in solving problems using production rules has not been made. It would be interesting to examine whether the error rate decreases with practice indicating transfer. It may help in designing of instruction programs based on production rule framework.

4. Mathematics education is a constant concern for general public. For the Visually Impaired in India, mathematics can be studied to the level, they can carryout the solutions mentally. It is not taught in higher classes because of the inability of the visually impaired child to carry out complex mathematical calculations. Thus, this task was appropriately chosen for the study. However, it was not possible to analyze the subskills to understand the nature of mathematical performance. It is suggestive, that, further research can be taken up, to account for the sequence and hierarchy of learning in mathematics so that the teachers and the curriculum designers can make sure that subskills that are preconditions can be acquired before the child can master complex procedures. Further research can also re—examine the procedures that can be attained easily and the ones that are difficult for the Visually Impaired in learning mathematics to use this in the design of instruction.

5. Learning and applying of knowledge to spatial tasks can be discriminative of Visually Impaired and sighted children. Research in this direction may be beneficial.

6. The study did not measure problem solving before providing training in production rules. A pilot study was suggestive of difficulties Visually Impaired children

faced in solving these problem tasks. The solutions they gave were segmentory and not hierachically organized. Further research may show the nature of solution procedures used before the training in production rule knowledge and compare it with procedures used after the training.

7. It could not be known from the study, that, for how long the subjects could sustain the learning. Further testing on the same problem after a time gap can show whether the subjects used the same logical rules, after a time gap or adopted some other system in solving problems.

8. The findings of the present study showed specific advantages of braille and audio medias of presentation. Further research, employing both the medias in a combined form, can show the effect of this on cognitive architecture of the Visually Impaired.

9. Lastly, it was not possible to get a representative sample of girls for the study because there is only one school for the blind girls in Delhi and the number of girls, after following the selection procedure, would have been very less to draw conclusions. Further research can discriminate between the features of cognitive architecture of Visually Impaired boys and girls.

6

SUMMARY

The domain of Cognition can be studied, using two approaches; the faculty approach that holds that distinct cognitive principles underlie the operation of distinct cognitive functions and the unitary approach that holds that all higher level cognitive functions can be explained by one set of principles. The study of cocgnitive architecture, based on unitary approach, is a study of relatively complete proposals about the structure of human cognition. It emphasizes that a single set of principles could explain a broad range of computational tasks likened to the modern general purpose computer.

Production Systems Architecture is one approach to study cognitive architecture. Production systems are defined as a class of computer simulation models that are stated in terms of condition — action rules that make strong ásumptions about the nature of cognitive architecture.

The motivations for production system architecture, as discussed, have been many. They are well structured, and guarantee that the behavior produced by learning them would be coherent. It is possible to delete or add production rules individually, which makes incremental learning definable. They are flexible, homogeneous, can combine parallel and serial coding and are goal driven. Thus, they have been found to be appropriate in the study of cognitive architecture, study of learning and learning mechanisms, acquisition of skills, solving of puzzles, transfer etc. Thus, they were selected to be the frameworks in the study of "Cognitive Axchitecture in the Visually Impaired".

Review of the Related Work

Studies show that production systems have been used to provide theoretical accounts of human performance on a variety of tasks ranging from adults behavior on various puzzles to children's responses to class — inclusion questions and learning.

Research on the acquisition of cognitive skills and intelligent tutoring, using the production systems has also been carried out by many researchers.

Objectives

The broad research questions evolving from the conceptualization of this study were regarding the features of cognitive architecture in the Visually Impaired and how these differs from that of sighted controls and which is the best media of presentation of information, in the absence of sight related to solving of various tasks which formed the framework of this study?

Methodology

The strategy generated for methodology involved Visually Impaired and Sighted children in the age range of 13-16 years, matched on intelligence, socio-economic background, syllabus in school, medium of instruction etc. On the basis of intelligence scores distribution 3 groups of Visually Impaired (2 high on intelligence and one low on intelligence) were selected and similarly, following the same criterion three groups of sighted controls were selected from government schools. The study was carried out in three parts, the pilot study, the training phase and the testing phase. Various tasks for training and testing purposes were selected and production systems were for malized on the basis of the pilot study.

Both the samples were given training using reading or listening as medias of presentation (Braille/print script or audio) in the use of production rules for solving six problems and then tested on similar but different twelve problems.

The production rules generated by them, in the solution of these problems, were analyzed on the basis of parameters known as response measures. These were

(a) Number of words

(b) Number of Rules

(c) Quality of Rules

(d) Time taken to learn the production systems

(e) Time taken to solve various problems using production rules

(f) Number of features

(g) Number of critical features

These response measures were' analyzed on the basis of vision status, intelligence and media of presentation.

The tasks involved in the training phase were: Mathematics, Pattern Matching, Balance Scale, Reasoning, Circle Formation and Animal Recognition.

The tasks involved in the testing phase were extension of the tasks above namely, Mathematics *I* and I, Pattern Matching Recognition I and II, Puzzle I and II, Reasoning I and II, Circle Formation I and Triangle Formation II, Animal Recognition I and II. The procedure involved training and testing all the subjects individually. In the training phase the subjects learned the production rules taking as much time as they wished. The criterion of mastery was, reproduction of a well formalised production rule from the systems he had just learned.

In the testing phase the sighted were blindfolded and all the subjects in both the groups were asked to solve twelve problems and verbalize the solution in terms of production ri4es as they solved tht.

Results

The results indicated the differences between Visually Impaired and Sighted children on some parameters in the functioning of cognitive architecture for some tasks. The Visually

Impaired subjects on the whole used more words to generate production systems though the difference was significant in only 4 tasks, but the word rate per unit of time was lower in the Visually Impaired as compared to the sighted controls.

The Visually Impaired differed from sighted controls in taking more time for learning and solving problems. On the parameters number 9f features and critical features and quality of production rules the Visually Impaired differed from Sighted controls on very few tasks indicating equivalence in functioning achieved by training in production rule models for similar tasks.

The high intelligence Visually Impaired differed from low intelligence in the same group for number of features for all the tasks and for critical features in ten out of twelve tasks, while the high intelligence sighted differed from low intelligence sighted on number of features for five tasks and on critical futures for three tasks only.

The high intelligence group in both the samples took lesser time in acquiring production rule models for various tasks as compared to low intelligence group.

The interaction effect between intelligence and vision status for number of words was significant for seven tasks and for time taken in training for only two tasks.

Media of presentation affected the number of rules in the Visually Impaired. They formulated more rules when trained through braille script. It also affected number of critical features in four tasks. The Visually Impaired used more critical features when trained through audio medium. No such difference was found in the sighted controls.

Discussion and suggestions for Further Research

The cognitive architecture of the visually impaired in the framework of present research is slower in functioning than that of the sighted based on the word rate employed, number of rules used and time taken to acquire production rule knowledge and time taken to solve various tasks, using the knowledge acquired in the training phase.

Though slow they can function at an equivalent level of the sighted children if they are trained or instructured in solving problem tasks using the production rule framework representing all the possible declarative and procedural knowledge related to these tasks.

Oral presentation was found to facilitate compiling of knowledge in fewer rules as compared to broille script presentation. However, braille script was effective in retrieving units of knowledge from the knowledge represented in Production Rules. Thus, no particular mode was found to be effective. A combination of both may be most effective in comprehending knowledge represented in Production Rules.

In the framework of limitations of the study, several suggestions for further research have been made including a strategy for training intervention i.e., intelligent tutoring system, follow up study to assess the knowledge sustained in production rules after a time gap, and studying the relationship of specific problem solving behavior with specific rules.

References

Abelson, R.P. 1981; Psychological States of the Script Concept. *American Psychologist* 36, 715-729.

Abravenel 1981; In Scholl (eds) *Foundations of Education for the Blind and Visually Handicapped Children and Youth.* Theory and Practice. American Foundation for the Blind. N.Y.

Anater, 1980; In Scholl *Foundations of Education for the Blind and Visually Handicapped Children and Youth.* Theory and Practice American Foundations for the Blind. N.Y.

Anderson D.W. 1984; Mental Imagery in Congenitally Blind Children. *Journal of Visual Impairment and Blindness,* May pp. 207—211.

Anderson, J.A. and Hinton G.E. 1981; Models of Information Processing in the Brain in G.E. Hinton and J.A. Anderson (eds.) *Parallel Models of Associative Memory.* Erlbaum, Hillsdale, N.J. pp. 9-48.

Anderson, J.R. 1976; *Language, Memory and Thought.* Hillsdale, N.J. Lawrence Erlbaum Associates.

Anderson, J.R. 1981; A Theory of Language Acquisition Based on General Learning Principles, *In Proceedings of the Seventh International Joint Conference on Artificial Intelligence,* pp. 165-170. Vancouver, B.C. Canada.

Anderson, J.R. 1981; *Cognitive skills and their Acquisition* Hillsdale, N.J. : Erlbaum.

Anderson, J.R. 1982; Acquisition of Cognitive Skill. *Psychological Review,* 89, 369-406.

Anderson, J.R, 1983; *The Architecture of Cognition* Cambridge, Mass: Harvard University Press.

Anderson, J.R. 1987; Skill Acquisition: Compilation of Weak Method Problem Solutions. *Psychological Review* 94: 192-210.

Anderson, J.R. 1990a; *The adaptive character of thought*. Hillsdale, N.J.: Eribaum.

Anderson, J.R. 1990b; *Cognitive Psychology and its Implications* (3rd ed.) New York: Freeman.

Anderson, J.R. 1992; Intelligent Tutoring and High School Mathematics. In *Proceedings of the Second International Conference on Intelligent Tutoring Systems* (pp 1-10). Montreal, Quebec, Canada.

Anderson, J.R., 1993; *Rules of the Mind,* Hillsdale. N.J. Erlbaum Associates.

Anderson J.R. 1993; Problem Solving and Learning. *American Psychologist,* 48, No.1, 35—44.

Anderson, J.R.; Boyle, C.F; Corbett, A; Lewis, M.W., 1990; Cognitive Modeling and Intelligent Tutoring, *Artificial Intelligence,* 42, 7-49.

Anderson, J.R., Boyle, C.F., Farell, R., Feiser, B. 1984; Cognitive Principles in the Design of Computer Tutors. In *Sixth Annual Conference of the Cognitive Science Program* (pp 2-16)

Anderson, J.R., Boyle, C.F., Reiser B.J. 1958; Intelligent tutoring systems. *Science,* 228, 456-462.

Anderson, J.R., Greeno, J.G., Kline, P.J. and Neves, D.M. 1981; Acquisition of Problem Solving Skill. In J.R. Anderson (ed.) *Cognitive Skills and Their Acquisition*. Hillsdale, N.J.: Lawrence Erlbaum Associates.

Anderson, J.R. and Jeffries, R., 1985; Novice LISP Errors Undetected Losses of Information from Working Memory; *Human—Computer Interaction,* 22, 403-423.

Anderson, J.R. Kline, P.J., Beasley, C.M., 1979; A Learning System and its Psychological Implications. *Proceedings of the Sixth International Joint Conference on Artificial Intelligence,* pp. 16-21. Tokyo, Japan.

Anderson, J.R. Kline, P.J., Beasley, C.M., 1978; *A Theory of Acquisition of Cognitive Skills,* Technical Report No. ONR 77-1. Department of Psychology, Yale University.

Anderson, J.R. Kline, P.J. and Lewis; 1977; A Production System Model for Language Processing, In P. Carpenter and M. Just (eds.) *Cognitive Processes in Comprehension.* Hillsdale; N.J.; Lawrence Erlbaum Associates.

Anderson, J.R. and Paulson, R. 1978; Interference in Memory for Pictorial Informaticn, *Cognitive Psychology,* 10, 178-202.

Anderson, J.R. and Reiser, B.J.; 1985; The LISP Tutor; *Byte,* 10, 159—175.

Anzai, Y. 1978; Learning Strategies by Compurer. Proceedings of *the Second Biennial Conference of the Canadian Society for Computational Studies of Intelligence,* pp. 181-190. Toronto, Ontario, Canada.

Anzai, Y. Mitsaya, Y. Nakajima, S. and Ura, 5. 1981; LPS: A Rule-based Schema — Oriented Knowledge Representation System. *Journal of Information Processing* 4, 177-185.

Anzai, Y. and Simon, H.A., 1979; The Theory of Learning by doing. *Psychological Review,* 86, 124-140.

Bailes, S.M. and Lambert, R.M. 1986; Cognitive Aspects of Haptic form Recognition by Blind and Sighted Subjects. *British Journal of Psychology.* 77, 451-58.

Baylor, G.W. Gascon, J., Lemoyne, G. and Pother, N. 1973; An Information Processing Model of Some Seriation Tasks, *Canadian Psychologist.* 14, 167-196.

Beni, R.D. and Cornoldi, C. 1988; Imagery Limitations in Totally Congenitally Blind Subjects *Journal or Experimental Psychology. Learning, Memory and Cognition.* Vol. 14, No.4, 650—655.

Bischoff, R.W. 1967; Improvement of Listening Comprehension in Partially Sighted Students: *Sight Saving Review.* Fall.

Bixler and Foualke E. 1963; Current Status of Research in Rapid Speech. *International Journal of Education of the Blind,* Dec (2).

Bobrow, D.G. and Winograd, T. 1977; An Overview of KRL, a Knowledge Representation Language, *Cognitive Science* 1, 3-46.

Boldt, W. 1969; The Development of Scientific Thinking in Blind Children and Adolescents. *Education of the Visually Handicapped,* 1(1), pp. 5-11.

Boring, E.G. 1950; *A History of Experimental Psychology* New York Appleton Century.

Brazdil, p. 1978; *Experimental Learning Model. Proceedings of the Third AISE GI Conference,* pp. 46-50. Hamburg, West Germany.

Breuer, Klaus and Kummer, Ruediger 1990; Cognitive Effects from Process Learning with Computer — based Simulations Special Issue: German Experimental Research in Learning and Instruction with Computers. *Computer in Human Behavior,* Vol. 6(1) 69—81.

Brown, J.S. and Van Lehn, K. 1980; Repair Theory: A Generative Theory of Bugs in Procedural Skill. *Cognitive Science, 4,* 379—427.

Burns H. 1988; Knowledge Based Educational Systems. *Aviation, Space and Environment* 59 (II, Suppl): 69-75.

Bushnell, W. 1981; The Ontogeny of Intermodal Relations. Vision and Infancy. In R.D. Walk and H.L. Pick (eds.) *Intersensory Perception and Sensory Integration.* New York, N.Y. Plenum Press.

Carbonell, J.G. 1983; Learning by Analogy: Formulating and Generalizing Plans from Past Experience. In R.S. Michalski J.G., Carbonell and T.M. Mitchell (Eds.) *Machine Learning* (pp.. 137-162). Paloalto, C.A. Tioga Press.

Card, S.K. Moran, T.P. and Newell, A., 1983; *The Psychology of Human Computer Interaction*. Hillsdale, N.J.: Eribaum.

Chase, W.G. and Ericsson, K.A. 1982; Skill and Working Memory. In G.H. Bower (Ed.), *The Psychology of Learning and Motivation* (Vol. 16). New York: Academic Press.

Chi, M.T.H., Glaser, R., Farr, M., 1988; (Eds). *The Nature of Expertise*. Hillsdale. N.J. Erlbaum.

Clark, H.H. 1974; Semantics and Comprehension, In R.A. Sebeok (Ed.) *Current Trends in Linguistics*. The Hague Monton.

Cobb, E.S. 1977; Learning Through Listening. A New Approach. *Journal of Visual Impairment and Blindness,* Sept., 71(7).

Daightery, K.M., 1974; Listening Skills, A Review of Literature, *New Outlook for the Blind*. 68(8), 68(9), 68(10).

Davjdson I.E.W.K. 1976; Studying Young Blind Children. *Orbit,* 33, 17—19.

Davis R. and King J. 1975; *"An Overview of Production Systems,"* AIM-271, The Artificial Intelligence Laboratory, Stanford University, Stanford, California.

Dorner, Dietrich and Kreuzig, Heinz W. 1983; Problem Solving Ability and Intelligence (Germ) *Psychological Rund Sehan (Oct),* Vol. 34(4), 185—192.

Dulany, D.E., Carlson, RA. and Dewey, GI., 1984; A Case of Syntactical Learning and Judgement. How Conscions and how Abstract ? *Journal of Experimental Psychology:* General, 113, 541—555.

Elio, R. and Anderson, J.R. 1984; The Effects of Information Order and Learning Mode on Schema Abstraction. *Memory and Cognition,* 12, 20-30.

Erikson, I. and King l.A. 1917; A Comparison of Visual and Oral Presentation of Lessons in the Case of Pupils from Third to Ninth Grade, *Schools and Society,* Aug 6.

Fikes R.E. and Nilsson N.J. 1971; "STRIPS: A New Approach to the Application of Theorem Proving to Problem Solving *Artif. Intell.* 2, 189—208.

Fodor, J.A. 1975; *The Language of Thought*. New York: Thomas Crowell.

Fodor, J.A. 1983; *The Modularity of the Mind*. Cambridge, Mass: MIT Press.

Fodor J.A. and Pylyshyn Z.N. 1988; Connectionism and Cognitive Architecture: A Critical Analysis. *Cognition* 28: 3—77.

Forgy, C.L. 1979a; *OPS4 User's Manual* Technical Report of Computer Science, Carnegie-Mellon University.

Forgy, C.L. 1979b; *On the Efficient Implementation of Production Systems* Dissertation. Department of Computer Science. Carnegie—Mellon University.

Forgy, C.L. 1981; *OPS5 User's Manual*. Technical Report Department of Computer Science. Carnegie -Mellon University.

Forgy, C.L. 1984; *The OPSB3 Report*. Technical Report. Department of Computer science. Carnegie—Mellon University.

Forgy C.L. and McDermott, J. 1976; *The OPS Reference Manual*, Technical Report Department of Computer Science, Carnegie— Mellon University.

Foulke. E. 1964; A Multisensory Test of Conceptual Ability. *New Outlook for the Blind*, 58, 75-77.

Gelman, R. and Gallistel, C.R. 1978; *The Child's Understanding of Number*, Cambridge, MA: Harvard University Press.

Gelman R. and Meck, E. 1983; Preschoolers Counting Principles Before Skill, *Cognition*, 13, 343-359.

Glaser R, 1988; Cognitive Science and Education, *International Journal of Social Science*. 115, pp. 21-43.

Goodman, R.M. Higgins, Charles M., Miller, John W and Smythe, Padhrajc, 1992; Rule-Based Neural Networks for Classification and Probability Estimation - *Neural Computation,* (NOV). Vol 4(6), 781-804.

Gore, G.V. III 1969; A Comparison of Two Methods of Speeded Speech, *Education of the Visually handicapped,* 1, (3).

Green and Raphael, 1968; Research on Intelligent Question An Swering Systems. *In Proceedings of the ACAl,* 169-181, Prinction Brandon Systems Press.

Hall 1981; In Scholl, G.T. (ed). *Foundations of Education for the Blind and Visually Handicapped Children and Youth.* Theory and Practice. American Foundation for the Blind. N.Y.

Halten, P. 1976, *Priorities in Educational Programs for Visually Handicapped Children and Youth.* DVH New Letter, Winter, 20(3).

Hayes-Roth, F. and McDermott. J. 1978; An Inference Matching Techniques for Inducing Abstractions, *Communications of the ACM21,* 401—410.

Hedrick, C. 1976; Learning Production Systems from Examples. *Artificial Intelligence* 7, 21—49.

Higgins, L.E. 1973; *Classification in Congenitally Blind Children,* (Research Series, No. 25) New York: American Foundations for the Blind, Inc.

Hollins N. 1985; Styles of Mental Imagery, *Neuropsychologia,* Vol. 23, No. 4, pp. 561—566.

Hunt E. 1989; Cognitive Science: Definition, Status, and Questions. *Annual Review of Psychology* 40: 603-29.

Hunter I.M.L. 1957; The Solving of Three Series Problem. *British Journal of Psychology,* 48, 268-298.

Hunter. I.M.L. 1968; Mental Calculation In P.C. Wason and P.N. Johnson-Laird (eds.) *Thinking and Reasoning* Baltimore Penguin Books.

Hull, C.L. 1952; *A behavior System. An Introduction to behavior Btheory Concerning the Individual Organism,* New Haven. Yale University Press.

Jeffries, R. Turner, A.A. Polson, P.G. Atwoods M.E. 1981; The Processes Involved in Designing Software. In J.R. Anderson (Ed.) *Cognitive Skills and Their Acquisition* (pp. 255-283), Hillsdale, N.J. Eribaum.

Karat. J. 1982. A Model of Problem Solving with Incomplete Constraint Knowledge. *Cognitive Psychology,* 14, 538-559.

Karrakar, M.E. 1952, An Evaluation of Influence of Interest and 'Set' on Listening Effectiveness in Basic Communication Class. *Speech Monographs.* 29: 117-18 (Abstract).

Katz, I.R. and Anderson, J.R. 1985; *An Exploratory Study of' Novice Programmers' Bugs and Debugging Behaviour.* Unpublished Manuscript.

Kieras, D.E., and Bovair, 5. 1986; The Acquisition of Procedures from Text A Production System Analysis of Transfer of Training. *Journal of Memory and Language.* 25, 507—524.

Kieras, D.E. and Polson, P.G. 1985; An Approach, to the Formal Analysis of User Complexity. *International Journal of Man-machine studies,* 22, 365-394.

Klahr, O. 1973; A Production System for Counting, Subitizing and Adding. In W.G. Chase (ed.) *Visual Information Processing* New York Academic Press.

Klahr, D., Langley, P., and Neches, R., 1987; *Production System Models of Learning and Development.* Cambridge. Mass MIT Press.

Klahr, D. and Siegler, R. 1978; The Representation of Children's Knowledge. In H. Reese and L.P. Lipsitt (eds.) *Advances in Child Development,* Vol.12, New York Academic Press.

Klahr, D. and Wallace, J.G. 1972; Class Inclusion Processes. In S. Farnham - Diggory (ed) *Information Processing in Children.* New York Academic Press.

Klahr, D. and Wallace, J.G. 1973; The Role of Quantification Operation in the Development of Conservation of Quantity. *Cognitive Psychology* 4. 301-327.

Klahr, D. and Wallace, J.G. 1976; *Cognitive Development*. An Information Processing View. Hillsdale. N.J.: Lawrence Erlbaum Associates.

Kline, P.J., 1983; *Computing the Similarity of Structured Objects by Means of a Heuristic Search for Correspondences*. Unpublished Doctoral Dissertation. University of Michigan. Ann Arbor.

Kohler, W. 1929; *The menlality of apes* New York: Mentality, Brace.

Kolers, P.A. and Smythe, W.E. 1984; "Symbol Manipulation Alternatives to Computational View of Mind." *Journal of Verbal Learning and Verbal behavior*, 23, 315-24.

Kotovsky, Hayes J.R., Simon, H.A. 1985; Why are Some Problems Hard? Evidence from Tower of Hanoi, *Cognitive Psychology*, 17, 248—294.

Laird, J.E. 1983; *Universal Subgoaling* Dissertation Department of Computer Science, Carnegie — Mellon University.

Laird, J.E., Rosenbloom, P.S. and Newell, A. 1984; Towards Chunking as a General Learning Mechanism. *In Proceedings of the National Conference on Artificial Intelligence*, pp. 173- 180. Toronto, Ontario, Canada.

Langley, P. 1978; BACON. 1: A General Discovery System. *Proceedings of the Second Biennial Conference of the Canadian Society for Computational Studies of Intelligence*, pp. 173-180. Toronto, Ontario, Canada.

Langley P. 1982; Language Acquisition Through Error Recovery. *Cognition and Brain Theory*, 5, 211-255.

Langley P. 1983; Learning Search Strategies Through Discrimination. *International Journal of Man-Machine Studies*, 18, 513—541.

Langley, P. and Neches, R.T. 1981; PRISM *User's Manual*. Technical Report. Computer Science Department, Carnegie— Mellon University.

Langley, P., Neches, R.T., Neves, D. and Anzai, Y. 1980; A Domain Independent Framework for Learning Procedures. *International Journal of Policy Analysis and Information Systems*. 4, 163—197.

Langley, P. Ohlsson, S. Thibadeau, R. and Walter, R. 1984; Cognitive Architectures and Principles of Behavior, *Proceedings of the Sixth Conference of the Cognitive Science Society*, pp. 244-247. Boulder, Colo.

Larkin, J.L. 1981; Enriching Formal Knowledge: A Model for Learning to Solve Textbook Physics Problems. In. J.R. Anderson (ed.) *Cognitive Skills and their Acquisition*. Hillsdale. N.J.: Lawrence Erlbaum Associates.

Larkin, J.H., McDermott, J., Simon, D.P. and Simon, H.A., 1980; Models of Competence in Solving Physics Problems. *Cognitive Science*, 4, 317—345.

Lenat, D.B. and Harris, G. 1978; Designing a Rule System that Search for Scienific Discoveries. In D.A. Waterman and F. Hayes-Roth, eds. *Pattern Directed Inference Systems*. New York: Academic Press.

Lesgold, A.M. 1984; Acquiring Expertise. In J.R. Anderson and S.M. Kosslyn (Eds.) *Tutorials in Learning and Memory* (pp.31-60) San Francisco: Freeman.

Lewis, C. 1978; *Productin System Models of Practice Effects*. Dissertation, Department of Psychlogy, University of Michigan.

Lewis, C. 1981; Skill in algebra. in J.R. Anderson (ed.) *Cognitive Skills and their Acquisition*. Hillsdale N.J.: Lawerence Erlbaum Associates.

Lewis, M.W. and Andersn, J.R. 1985; Discrimination of Operator Schemeta in Problem Solving. Learning from Examples. *Cognitive Psychology*, 17, 26-65.

Malin, A. 1966; *Adaptation of Weschsler's Intelligence Scale for Children*. Doctoral Thesis, Nagpur University.

McCarthy, J. 1956; The Inversion of Functions Defined by Turing Machines. in C.E. Shanon & J. McCarthy (Eds.) *Automata Studies, Annals of Mathematics Studies*, 34, 177-181, Princeton, N.J., Princeton University.

McClelland, J.L. and Rumelhart, D.E. 1981; An Interactive Model of Context Effects in Letter Perception: Part I. An Account of Basic Findings. *Psychological Review*. 88., 253-264.

McClelland, J.L. and Rumelhart, D.E. (Eds.) 1986; *Parallel Distribution Processing ; Explorations in the Microstructure of Cognition. Vol.2., Psychological and Biological. Models,* Cambridge, Mass., MIT Press.

McCulloch, W.S. and Pitts, W. 1943; A Logical Callulus of the Ideas Immanent in Nervous Activity. *Bulletin of Mathematical Biophysics,* Vol. 4, pp. 115-33.

McDermott, J. 1979; Learning to use Analogies. *Proceedings of the Sixth International Joint Conference on Artificial Intelligence,* pp. 568-576, Tokyo, Japan.

McDermott, D. and Doyle, J. 1980; Non-monotonic Logic. *Artificial Intelligence,* 13, 41—72.

McKendree, J. and Anderson, J.R. (in press). Frequency and Practice Effects on the Composition of Knowledge in USP Evaluation. In J.M. Carroll (Ed.) *Cognitive Aspects of humazi Computer Interaction.*

Michalski, R.S. 1980; Pattern Recognition as Rule-guided Inductive Inference. *IEEE Transctions on Pattern Analysis and Machine Intelligence,* 2, 349-361.

Millar, S. 1981; Cross Modal and Intersensory Perception and the Blind, in R.D. Walk and H.L. Picks (eds.) *Intersensory Sensory Integration,* New York, N.Y.: Plenum Press.

Miller, G.A.; Galanter. E.; Pribram, K., 1960; *Plans and Structure of Behaviour.* New York: Holt. Rinehart and Winston.

Minsky. M.L. 1967; *Computation Finite and Infinite Machines* Englewood Cliffs, N.J.: Prentice - Hall.

Minsky, M.L. 1975; "A Framework for Representing Knowledge" in the *Psychology of Computer Vision,* ed. P.H. Winston, New York; Mc Graw-Hill.

Mitchell, T.M., Utgoff, P. and Banerji, R.B. 1983; Learning Problem Solving Heurustics by Experimentation. In R.S. Michalski, J.G. Carbonell and T.M. Mitchell (eds.) *Machine Learning an Artificial Intelligence Approach.* Palo Alto, Calif. Tioga Publishing.

Montare, A. 1992; Knowledge Acquisition from Learning Procedural Cognition and its Declarative Cognizance *Perceptual and Motor Skills* Jan. pp. 243—257.

Neches. R. 1981a.; A Computational Formalism for Heuristic Procedure Modification. *Proceedings of the Seventh International Joint Conference on Artificial Intelligence,* pp. 283-288. Vancouver, B.C. Canada.

Neches. R. 1981b; *Models of Heuristic Procedure Modification.* Department of Psychology. Carnegie-Mellon University.

Neches, R. Langley, P. Klahr, D. 1987; Learning Development and *Production Systems In Production System and Models of Learning and Development* ed. D. Klahr P. Langley, R. Neches, Cambridge Mass.

Nesher, P. 1986; Learning Mathematics, A Cognitive Perspective *American Psychologist,* Vol. 41, No. 10, pp. 1114—1122.

Neves, D.N. 1978; A Computer Program that Learns Algebric Procedures by Examining Examples and Working Problems in a Textbook *Proceedings of the Second Bieninal Conferene of the Canadian Society for Computational Studies of Intelligence* pp. 191-195. Toronto, Ontario, Canada.

Neves, D.M. and Anderson, J.R. 1981; Knowledge Compilation Mechanism for the Automatization of Cognitive Skills. In J.R. Anderson (ed.) *Cognitive Skills and their Acquisition.* Hillsdale, N.J.: Erlbaum Associates.

Newell, A. 1967; Studies in Problem Solving. *Subject 3 on the Crypt Arithmetic Task Donald + Gerald = Robert* Technical Report. Centre for the Study of Information Processing. Carnegie Institute of Technology.

Newell. A. 1970; Remarks on the Relationship Between Artificial Intelligence and Cognitive Psychology, in R. Banerji and M.D. Mesarovic (eds). *Theoretical Approaches to Non-Numerical Problem Solving,* Springer-Verlag, New York.

Newell, A. 1973; Production Systems. Models of Control Structures. In W.G. Chase (ed.) *Visual Information Processing.* New York: Academic Press.

Newell, A. 1980; Reasoning, Problem Solving and Decision Processes. The Problem Space Hypothesis. In R. Nickerson (ed.) *Attention and Performance.* Vol. 8. Hillsdale. N.J. Lawrence Erlbaum Associates.

Newell. A. 1982; "The Knowledge level" *Artificial Intelligence,* 1887—127.

Newell, A. and McDermott, J. 1975; *PSG Manual,* Technical Report. Department of Computer Science, Carnegie-Mellon University.

Newell, A. and Rosenbloom, P.s. 1987; Mechanism of Skill Acquisition and the Law of Practice. In J.R. Anderson (ed.) *Cognitive Skills and Their Acquisition,* Hillsdale. N.J. Lawerence Erlbaum Associates.

Newell, A. Shaw, J.C. Simon, H.A. 1958; Elements of a Theory of Human Problem Solving *Psychological Review,* Vol. 65, pp. 151—66.

Newell, A. and Simon, H.A. 1961a; GPS, a Program that Stimulates Human Thought in H. Billing (ed). *Lernende Automaten,* 109-124. Munchan: R. Oldenbourg.

Newell, A. and Simon, H.A. 1972; *Human Problem Solving* Englewood Cliffs. N.J.: Prentice Hall.

Nolan, C.Y., Brothers R.T., Morris, J.K., 1973; Guide to Effective Study Through Listening. *In Rural Study, Systems for the Visually Handicapped.* New York. Recording for the Blind.

Noorodman, L. G.M. 1977; *Inferring from Language.* Dissertation. Rijksuniversiteit to Groningen.

Norman, D.A., 1981; Categorization of Action Slips. *Psychological Review,* 88, 1-15.

Norman, D.A. and Rumelhart, 1975; *Explorations in Cognition.* San Francisco. W.H. Freeman.

Ohlsson, 5. 1979; PSS3 *Reference Manual.* Working Paper Number 4. Cognitive Seminar Department. of Psychology, University of Stockholm.

Ohlsson. S. 1980a; *A Possible Path to Expertise in the Three Term Series Problem.* Technical Report, Department of Psychology, University of Stockholm.

Ohlsson, S. 1980b. *Competence and Strategy in Reasoning with Common Spatial Concepts.* A Study of Problem Solving in a Semantically Rich Domain. Dissertation, Departiment of Psychology, University of Stockholm.

Ohlsson. S. 1983; A Constrained Mechanism for Procedural Learning. *In Proceedings of the Eighth International Joint Conference on Artificial Intelligence,* pp. 426-428. Karlsruhe. West Germany.

Oswald, Margit, Gadenne and Volker 1984; Knowing How, Knowing that and AI: An Analysis of the Concept of Declarative and Procedural Knowledge (Germ) *Sprache and Kognition,* (July), Vol. 3(3), 173—184.

Paknikar, K.K. 1978; *Performance Tests For the Blind.* NAB Workshop for the Blind. Bombay.

Patrick, Henry and Winston. 1977; *Artificial Intelligence,* Addison wesley Pub. Comp.

Piaget, J. 1952; *The Child's Conception of Number.* New York Norton (Original Work Published in French, 1941).

Pirolli, P.L. and Anderson, J.R., 1984; *The Role of Mental Models in Learning to Program:* Paper Presented at the Twenty-fifth Annual Meeting of the Psychonomic Society, San antonia Tx.

Polson, M. and Richardson, J. 1988; (Eds.) *Handbook of Intelligent Training Systems.* Hillsdale, N.J. Erlbaum.

Post, E.L. 1943; Format Reductions of the General Combinatorial Decision Problem. *American Journal of Mathematics*. 65, 197-268.

Pylyshyn, Z.W. 1984; *Computation and Cognition*. Towards a Foundation for Cognitive Science. Cambridge Mass MIT Press.

Rai, N.K. 1987; Comprehension of Visually Handicapped Children Using Audio and Tactile Media; A Comparison. *Indian Journal of Disability and Rehabilitation*. Jan-June.

Reber, A.S. 1976; Implicit Learning of Synthetic Languages. The Role of Instructional Set. *Journal of Experimental Psychology: Human Learning and Memory*. 2, 88-94.

Resnick, L.B. and Omanson S.F. (in press) Learning to Understand Arithmetic. In R. Glaser (Ed.) *Advances in Instructional Psychology* (Vol 3) Hillsdale, N.J. Erlbaum.

Riley, M.S. and Greeno, J.G. 1980; *Details of Programming a Model of Children's Counting in ACTP*. Pittsburgh Learning Research and Development Centre.

Rosenbloom, P.S. 1979; *XAPS Reference Manual*. Technical Report. Department of Computer Science, Carnegie — Mellon University.

Rubin, E.J. 1964; *Abstract Functioning in the Blind* New York American Foundation for the Blind, Inc.

Rumelhart, D.E. and McClleland J.L. (eds.) 1986; *Parallel Distributed Processing: Exploration in the Microstructure of Cognition. Vol. 1: Foundations*. Cambridge. Mass: MIT Press.

Rumelhart, D.E. and Ortony, A. 1976; The Representation of Knowledge in Memory, In R.C. Anderson, R.J. Spiro and W.E. Montague (ed.). *Schooling and the Acquisition of Knowledge* Hillsdale, N.J. Eribaum Associates.

Rychener, M.P. 1976; *Production Systems As A Programming Language for Artificial Intelligence Applications*. Dissertation, Department of Computer Science. Carnegie- Mellon University.

Rychener, M.D. 1980; *OPSS Production System Language. Tutorial and Reference Manual.* Unpublished Manuscript. Department of Computer Science. Carnegie—Mellon University.

Sacerdoti, E.D. 1977; *A. Structure for Plans and Behavior.* New York: Elsevier North-Holland.

Santin, S., Nesker. and Simmons. J., 1977; Problems in the Construction of Reality in Congenitally Blind Children. *Journal of Visual Impairment and Blindness.*, 71, 425-429.

Sauers, R. and Farrell, R. 1982; *GRAPES user's Manudl* Technical Report. Department of Psychology. Carnegie-Mellon University.

Schank R.C. and Abelson, R.P. 1977. Scripts, Plans, Goals and Understanding, Erlbaum, Hillsdale, N.J. 1977.

Schneider, W. and Shiffrin, R.M. 1977; Controlled and Automatic Human Information Processing I. Detection, Search and Attention. *Psychological Review*, 84, 1-66.

Scholl, G.T. 1973; *Foundation of Education for the Blind and Visually Handicapped Children and Youth. Theory and Practice.* Americn Foundation for the Blind. N.Y.

Shannon, C.E., 1950; "Programming a Computer for Playing Chess." *Philosophical Magazine* 41: 256-275.

Shehan P.W. and Jilden J. 1983; Effects of Suggestibility and Hypnosis on Accurate and Distorted Retrieval from Memory. *Journal of Experimental Psychology. Learning, Memory, Cognition,* Vol. 9, No. 2, 283-293.

Shortliffe, T. and Buchanan, B. 1975; A model of Exact Reasoning in Medicine. *Mathematical Bio-sciences.* 23, 351-374.

Siegler, R.S. and Shrager, J. 1983; May Strategy Choices in Addition *How Children Know What to do.* Paper Presented at the 18th Annual Carnegie Symposium on Cognition, Pittsburgh, P.A.

Simon, D.P. and Simon, H.A. 1978; Individual Differences in Solving Physics Problems. In R. Siegler (ed.) *Children's Thinking: What Develops?* Hillsdale. N.J.: Lawrence Erlbaum Associates.

Singley, M.K. and Anderson, J.R., 1985; The Transfer of Text-Editing Skill. *Journal of Man-Machine Studies, 22*, 403-423.

Smolensky, P. 1986; 'Information Processing in Dynamical, Systems: Foundations of Harmony Theory - In D.E. Rumelhart, J.L. McClleland and PD P Research Group (eds.) *Parallel Distributed Processing: Explorations in the Micro-Structure of Cognition* (Vol.1) Cambridge, Mass: Bradford Books.

Spilabury, Georgina, Stankov, Lazar and. Roberts, Richards, 1990; The Effect of Test's Difficulty on its Correlation with Intelligence *Personality and Individual Differences*, 1990, Vol. 11(10) 1069—1077.

Stenberg, R.J. Guyote, M.J. and Turner, M.E. 1980; Deductive reasoning. In R.E. Snow, P.A. Federico and W.E. Montague (eds.) *Aptitude Learning and Instruction*, Vol. 1, Hillsdale, N.J.: Lawerence Erlbaum Associates.

Stephens and Grube 1982; In Scholl, G.T. (ed). *Foundations of Education for the Blind and Visually Handicapped Children and Youth. Theory and Practice.* American Foundation for the Blind. N.Y.

Thibadeau. R. 1982; CAPS: A Language for Modeling Highly - Skilled Knowledge Intensive Behavior. *Proceedings of the National Conference on the use of On-line Computers in Psychology*. Minneapolis Minn.

Thibadeaus, R. Just. M.A. ad Carpenter, P.A. 1983; A Model of the Time Course and Content of Reading *Cog. Sc.* 6 157—203.

Thorndike, E. 1898; Animal Intelligence: An Experimental Study of the Associative Processes n Animals. *Psychological Review, Monograph Supplement*, 2 (2 Whone No. 8).

Thorndike, E.L. 1903; *Educational Psychology*. New York. Lemke and Buechner.

Tolman, E.C. 1932; *Purposive Behavior in Animals and Men* New York. Appleton - Century-Crofts.

Turing, A.M. 1937; "On Computable Numbers with an Application to the Entscherdungs *Proceedings of the London Mathematical Society* 42 230-265.

Turing, A.M. 1950; "Computing Machinery and Intelligence," in *Mind,* reprinted 1964 in Minds and Machines, ed. A.R. Anderson. Englewood Cliffs, N.J. Prentice - Hall.

Vakali, M. 1984-85; Children's Thinking in Arithmetic Word Problem Solving. *Journal of Experimental Education,* pp. 106-113.

Van Lehn, K. 1983; *Felicity Conditions for Human Skill Acquisition Validating on AI - based Theory.* (Tech. Rep. No. CIS-21) Palo alto CA Xerox Parc.

Van Lehn, K. 1988. Problem-Solving and Cognitive Skill acquisition In M. Posner (Ed.) *The Foundations of Cognitive Science* (pp. 527—580) Cambridge. MA MIT Press.

Vanderplas and Garvin 1959a; In Sidowski, J.B., (eds.) *Experimental Methods and Instrumentation in Psychology,* McGraw Hill Inc.

Von Neumann, J., 1966; "Rigorous Theories of Control and Information," in *Theory of Self—Reproducing Automata,* Urbana Univ. of Illinois Press, pp. 42—56.

Voronin, V.M. 1985; *Psychological Pedagogical Aspects of Teaching Visually Impaired School children with the Help of Computers.* (Russ), Defeklogiya, No.1, 49—56.

Waldrop, M. 1988; Toward a Unified Theory of Cognition, *Science* Vol 241 (461), 27—29.

Wason, P.C. and Johnson-Laird, P.N. 1972; *Psychology of Reasoning Structure and Content.* Cambridge. MA Harvard Univ. Press.

Wason, P.C. and Shapiro, D. 1971; Natural and Contrived Experience in a Reasoning Problem, *Quarterly Journal of Experimental Psychology,* 23, 63-71.

Waterman, D.A. 1970; Generalization Learning Techniques for Automating the Learning of Heuristics. *Artificial Intelligence* 1, .121—170.

Waterman, D.A. 1975; Adaptive Production Systems. *Proceedings of the fourth International Joint Conference on Artificial Intelligence*. pp. 296—303. Tbilisi, USSR.

Wills, D.M. 1965; Some Observations on Blind Nursery School Children;s Understanding of Their World. *Psychoanalytic Study of the Child* New York International University Press.

Winston, P.H. 1975; Learning Structural Descriptions from Examples. In P.H. Winston (ed.) *The Psychology of Computer Vision*. New York McGraw Hill.

Witkin, H.A. and Associates 1968; Cognitive Pattering in Congenitally Totally Blind Children. *Child Development*, 39 (3), pp. 767—786.

Witkin, H.A. Ottman, P.K., Chase, J.B. and Friedman, F. 1971; Cognitive Patterning in the Blind. In J. Helmuth (ed.) *Cognitive Studies-Deficits in Cognition*. New York, N.Y. Brunner—Mazer.

Young. R.M. 1976; *Seriation by Children. An Artificial Intelligence Analysis of a Piagetian Task*. Basel Birkhauser.

Young, R.M. 1979; Production Systems for Modeling Human Cognition. In D. Michie (ED) *Expert Systems in the Microelectronic age*. Edinburgh Edinburgh University Press, pp. 35—45.

Index

A

Acquisition of knowledge, 37
ACT, 12, 13, 14, 15
ACT learning mechanisms, 25
ACT production system, 13, 22
ACT theory, 15, 22, 23
ACTE, 13
ACTF, 12, 13
ACTG, 12
ACTH, 12
Anderson, 2, 17, 19
Anderson, David W., 32
Anderson, J.R., 3, 20, 21, 23
Animal recognition, 51, 104, 105
ANOVA, 77
Application, 14
Arithmeticword problems, 27
Artificial intelligence, 3

B

Bailes, Sally M., 32
Baylor, 18
Beni, Rossana De, 32
Blind children, 32
– chlordane, 31
– pupils, 31

C

CAPS, 12
Carnegie-Mellon University, 12
Changes occurring due to child development, 26
Charles, M., 16
Classical architectures, 2
Classical method of the mind, 3
Cognitive analysis, 36
Cognitive architecture, 2-4
  advantages of production rules as cognitive architectures, 8-9
    goal-driven behaviour, 8
    homogeneity, 8
    independence, 8
    modeling memory, 9
    parallel/serial nature, 8
    stimulus-response flavor, 8
  collection of productions defines a tree of conclusions, 7
  creating new rules, 20
  development of production system architecture programming, 11
  different production system, 11
  domain of the cognition, 3
  features of production system, 5-8
    act process, 6
    conflict resolution process, 6
    match process, 6
    matching production rules, 6

framework of production system, 10
further implications for instructions: intelligent tutoring, 24
history of production rules, 9-10
information of processing system, 2
knowledge compilation process, 21
loss of vision is regarded to be the most damaging of any sensory loss, 29
other cognitive architectures, 15-17,
production memory and working memory, 6
– system architecture to study specific skills/problems, 2528
– – architecture, 4-5
learning mechanisms, 18, 19
skill acquisition, 20-23
review of the related studies, 17-34
history of research on production system, 17-18
production system architecture, 18
studies comparing visually impaired and sighted, 28-34
techniques of rule modification, 19
Cognitive development, 31
– patterning in congenitally totally blind children, 30
– science, 35
– skills, 35
Computation and cognition, 2
Computational view, 1
Computer programme, 2
Concept of symbol, 2
Current state, 5

D

Davidson, 32
Description of the training tasks, 51-54
Development of concepts, 31
Discussion, limitations and suggestions for further research, 110-120
ACT production system model, 115
artificial intelligence, 115
general picture, 112
mathematics task the visually impaired, 116
media of presentation, 112
– – training whether audio or Braille script, 117
observation, 117
organization of language, 110
overall picture, 114
programming of knowledge or collapsing the productions, 111
visually impaired children, 113
visual system is impaired or completely, 114
word rate employed, 110
Domain of cognition, 121

E

Education of the visually impaired two primary communication modes, 37
Elementary information processes (EIP), 3
Emphasis on integrated education, 37
EPAM, 17

F

Features of cognitive architecture, 118
Features of production system, 9
Fodor, J.A., 3
Formalisms of computer science and mathematics, 9
Formation of the intellectual structures, 31

G

Gascon, 18
General problem solver in 1957, 4
Goodman, 16
GRAPES, 12

H

Hand-simulation, 17
Higgins, 16
Hollins, Mark, 33
Human cognition, 4
Hunt, Earl, 2

I

Information processing, 1
Intelligence Scale for Indian Children (ISIC), 50
Intelligence, 39
Introduction, 1-34
IPS, 3

J

Jeffries, 23
Jilden, Jan, 34
John, W., 16

K

Klaher and Siegler model, 53
Klahr, David, 5

L

Lack of vision, 31
Lambert, Robert M., 32
Langley, P., 5, 19, 28
Learning, 119
Lemoyne, 18
Lewis, M.W., 23
LISP evaluation skills, 22
LISP tutor, 21
Listening, 37
Low intelligence group, 104

M

Major components of schema framework, 15
Mathematical problem, 51
Mathematics education, 119
Media of presentation, 39, 92
    ANOVA with media presentation and vision status, 93-99
Memory capacity, 23
Methodology, 39-57
    balance scale task, 53
    circle formation test, 52
    data-flow network for discussion of pattern matching, 53
    design, 42-44
        intelligence, 45
        media of presentation, 45
        parameters designated as response measures, 45
        vision status, 45
    hypotheses, 47
        intelligence, 47
        media of presentation, 49
        vision status 47
    materials and tasks, 50
    objectives, 40-46
    pattern matching production, 52
    procedure, 55-57
        instructions, 56
        instructions, 57

pilot study, 55
teuting, 56
training, 56
sample, 46
tasks for testing, 54-55
animal recognition, 55
circle formation and triangle formation, 55
maths, 54
pattern matching, 54
puzzles, 54
reasoning, 55
verbalize the production system, 40
visually impaired population, 46
Millar, 16, 29
Mitchell, H., 7
Model of counting, 26
Montre, 28
Motivation for production system architecture, 121

N

Neches, Robert, 5
Neoclassical, 10
Nesher, Pearla, 26
Neuman, John Von, 3
Newell, 2, 11

O

Objective, 37-38
OPS. 12

P

Padhriac, 16
Pattern matching, 106, 107
Performance, 14
Physical theories, 1
Pother, 18
PRISM, 12
Problem solving, 35
Problem, 35-38
Production matching, 14
Production system models of learning and development, 5
PSG, 11
Psychology, 4
Puzzle, 106
Pylyshyn, Z.W., 2, 3

R

Reading, 37
Representational theories, 2
Research on the acquisition of cognitive skills, 21
Response measures, 58
ANOVA with intelligence and vision status, .79-82
critical features, 59
difference between means on number of critical features, 78-79
– – – on visually impaired and sighted children, 76-77
– – – – on quality of productions of visually impaired, 75
– – – – on the taken to solve the problem tasks by visually impaired, 83
findings, 104-108
high and low intelligence visually impaired group, 84-91
intelligence, 54
interaction bet. vision status, 66-71
number of features employe, 59, 102
number of rules, 58
– – words, 58
problem takes in the testing phase, 73, 74
– – during training phase, 92

quality of production rules, 58
rules used by visually impaired trained by Braille/audio, 100
summary ANOVA with intelligence and vision status, 60-65
time taken in training and solving problems, 59
vision status, 59
word rate employed/unit of time by visually impaired and sighted children, 72
Results, 58-109
Review of the related work, 122
Rodney, M., 16
Rules of the mind, 24

S

Shehan, W., 34
Short-term memory (STM), 3
Sighted children, 50
Simon, 2, 17
Smythe, 16
SOAR, 13
Solution of tasks, 55
Solving problem, 119
Storage, 14

T

Teaching mathematical procedures, 26
Tower of Hanoi problem, 27
Traditional pre-experimental view, 1
Training material, 37
Transition mechanisms, 35

U

Unitary mental system, 4
Use of computer, 1

V

Vakali, Mary, 27
Various tasks, 55
Vision status, 39
Visual impairment on cognitive development, 30
Visually impaired children, 99
Visually impaired, 73

W

Waldrop, Mitchell, 5
WHO, 36
Working memory, 13